BUILD
YOUR
AUDIENCE

BUILD YOUR AUDIENCE

The 60-day traffic attraction playbook to increase your leads and sales as a writer, coach, or speaker

Jonathan Milligan

PGB

PLATFORM GROWTH BOOKS

Book Cover by Platform Growth Books

Illustrations by Jonathan Milligan

1st edition 2024

YOUR FREE GIFT

As a way of saying thanks for your purchase, we are offering a free companion online course called, *The Build Your Audience Accelerator Course.*

With this companion online course, you'll be able to fully implement all the exercises, worksheets, and checklists inside this book. To get free instant access, go to:

MarketYourMessage.com/build-course

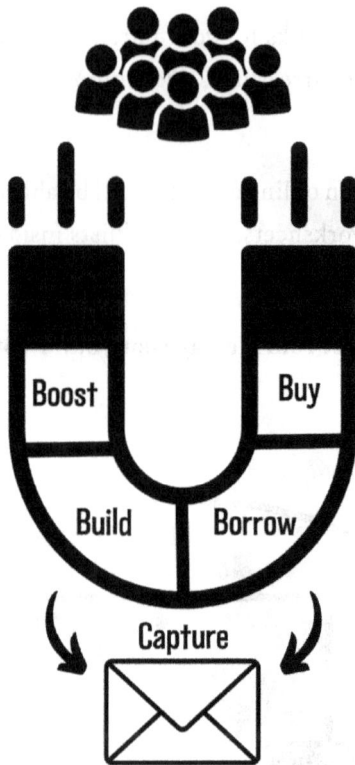

The Audience Attraction Playbook

Inside the pages of this book, you'll discover a powerful framework known as the Audience Attraction Playbook. To build your audience, you need clarity on five key elements: Capture (your lead magnet), Boost (your social media engagement), Build (your evergreen content), Borrow (your partnership strategies), and Buy (your paid advertising).

Contents

Introduction

Y ou're the best-kept secret online.

Years ago, a customer spoke those words to me. They meant it as a compliment. But their words hit me like a punch to the gut. They meant well, but all I heard was "invisible." Who was I to think anyone would care what I had to say? Maybe I wasn't expert enough. Maybe my message wasn't polished enough. The self-doubt was crippling.

But here's the truth: You don't need to be a secret to be valuable.

Over the years, I've discovered that building an audience isn't about being the loudest or the smartest. It's about being authentic and strategic. And I've developed a 60-day system that can help anyone - yes, even you - go from best-kept secret to can't-miss authority.

Imagine logging into your social media. You see real engagement: comments, shares, and messages from people whose lives you've touched. Picture your inbox filling up with speaking requests and collaboration opportunities. Envision launching your next project to an eager audience who can't wait to support you.

That's the power of strategic audience building. This isn't about gimmicks or manipulative tactics. It's about connecting with the right people in the right way. I've used these exact strategies to transform from a hidden secret to a recognized expert, and I've helped countless others do the same.

In "Build Your Audience," I'm pulling back the curtain and giving you my step-by-step playbook. This book is for you if you want to be a thought leader, author, or coach. It will show you how to package your expertise and attract your ideal audience.

No more best-kept secret.

No more waiting to be "discovered."

No more feeling like an imposter.

Just a clear, actionable plan to build your platform and amplify your message.

So, if you're ready to step out of the shadows and into the spotlight, you're in the right place. Let's turn your expertise into impact and your passion into a thriving platform.

Your journey from hidden secret to shining star starts now. Are you ready to be seen?

1

The Audience Attraction
Playbook

In a world of flashy ads and aggressive sales pitches, Blendtec was just another face in the crowd. It was 2006, and this humble blender company struggled to make waves in a sea of kitchen appliances.

Then, marketing director George Wright had an epiphany. What if they could show off their blenders' power in a way that was so outrageous and entertaining that people couldn't help but watch?

Enter "Will It Blend?" - a YouTube series that took the internet by storm. iPhones, golf balls, even a garden rake - nothing was safe from the whirring blades of a Blendtec blender. As chunks of marble and shards of electronics flew, so did the view counts. Millions tuned in, not to watch a product demonstration but to see what crazy item would meet its demise next.

The genius? Blendtec never once asked viewers to buy. They didn't have to. The videos spoke for themselves, showcasing the blenders' power in a way no traditional ad ever could. This wasn't push marketing; this was pull marketing at its finest.

The result? A staggering 700% increase in sales over three years. Blendtec transformed from an unknown brand to a household name, all because they dared to entertain rather than sell.[1]

This is the power of attraction marketing, the art of pulling customers in rather than pushing products out. It's about making content so valuable that your excited audience comes to you.

This chapter will unpack the Audience Attraction Playbook. We'll see why building relationships is better than chasing sales. A pull marketing approach can revolutionize your business.

So, put away your sales scripts and reduce the volume of those promotional ads. It's time to learn how to become the magnet that naturally draws your ideal audience to you. Are you ready to blend your way to success?

The Outdated Push: Why Traditional Marketing Falls Short

Let's examine what most people do when it comes to marketing. They seem to be stuck in a time warp, still using tactics from the era of door-to-door vacuum salesmen.

They're obsessed with optimizing sales funnels. Every click, page view, and interaction is scrutinized and tweaked to squeeze out just one more sale. It's all about the numbers, baby. Conversion rates, average order value, and customer acquisition cost are their gods.

And let's remember the holy grail: immediate revenue. Who cares about building relationships when you can make a quick buck now? They're playing a game called "How fast can we get this person to whip out their credit card?"

Then, there are the aggressive "push" marketing tactics. You know the type—those flashy ads that scream "BUY NOW!" or the relentless email campaigns that flood your inbox. It's the digital equivalent of a used car salesman in a loud plaid jacket pushing you to sign on the dotted line.

But here's the kicker - this approach is about as effective as trying to push a rope.

First, it creates discomfort. Think about it. What's your reaction when you walk into a store, and a salesperson immediately pounces on you? You probably want to turn tail and run. The same principle applies online. Push too hard, and you'll push people right out of your digital door.

Secondly, this approach ignores a crucial fact that marketing guru Dean Jackson uncovered. His study found that a whopping 85% of buyers make their purchase decision after 90 days. Could you let that sink in? By focusing solely on immediate sales, you could ignore 85% of your future customers. It's like leaving money on the table - lots of it.

Lastly, this short-sighted approach sacrifices long-term growth for short-term gains. Sure, you might make a few quick sales, but at what cost? You're burning bridges faster than you can build them. You're trading the possibility of lifelong customers for one-time buyers.

It's like the business equivalent of fast food. Sure, it might satisfy your hunger for immediate revenue, but it's not doing your business any favors in the long run. You're left unsatisfied, your customers feel used, and your business's health needs to improve.

So, what's the alternative if this is what most people do, and it doesn't work? Buckle up because we're about to flip the script on everything you thought you knew about marketing. It's time to stop pushing and start pulling. Are you ready to become a customer magnet?

Pull Marketing: The Customer Magnet Strategy

Have you ever watched a magnet attract metal shavings? That's pull marketing in action. You're not chasing customers; you're drawing them in.

Valuable content is your secret weapon. Blog posts, videos, podcasts - whatever floats your boat. The key? Make it helpful, make it interesting, make it shareable.

Think about the last time you encountered a really useful piece of content. Maybe it solved a problem you'd been grappling with, or it taught you something new. How did you feel about the person or company that created it? I bet you were pretty grateful, right?

That's the power of pull marketing. You're building goodwill, establishing trust, and becoming a go-to resource.

Here's a radical idea: forget about selling for a minute. I'd like you to focus on helping instead. Answer questions, solve problems, and share insights.

It's like dating. You don't propose on the first date, do you? No, you get to know each other first, and then you build a relationship. The same goes for marketing.

Create content that acts like a magnet. Make it so good that people can't help but be drawn to you. They'll come for the content but stay for the relationship.

And when the time comes to make an offer? They're already primed to say yes. Because you've already proven your value. You've already shown that you understand their needs.

Remember: pull marketing isn't about immediate gratification. It's about playing the long game. But the payoff? It's worth its weight in gold.

Capture: Building Your Email List

Your email list is your digital gold mine. It's a direct line to your audience, free from algorithm changes or platform shifts.

Think of your email list as a garden. You plant seeds (attract subscribers), nurture them (provide value), and watch them grow (build relationships). It takes time, but the harvest is worth it.

Want to attract subscribers? Use lead magnets. Offer something valuable in exchange for an email address—an ebook, a checklist, a mini-course—make it irresistible.

Lead magnets work because they provide immediate value. They're like a free sample at the grocery store. Does it taste good? If so, you'll probably buy the product.

Boost: Increasing Social Media Engagement

Social media isn't just for cat videos and food pics. It's a powerful tool for visibility and connection.

Matt Goulart nailed it: "Social media is about the people! It's not about your business. Provide for the people, and the people will provide for you."

Focus on value-driven content. Share insights, ask questions, and start conversations. Treat your followers like friends, not potential customers.

Want more engagement? Be engaging. Respond to comments. Join discussions. Show the human behind the brand.

Build: Creating Evergreen Content

Evergreen content is the gift that keeps on giving. It attracts traffic long after you've hit publish.

Pick your preferred method for blogs, podcasts, YouTube videos, Medium articles, and Pinterest pins. The key is to make it discoverable and valuable over time.

SEO is your secret weapon. It's how people find your content months or years later. Use relevant keywords, but don't stuff them in. Write for humans first, search engines second.

Think of Benjamin Franklin's Poor Richard's Almanac. It was packed with helpful information, witty sayings, and weather forecasts, and people looked forward to it each year. That's evergreen content in action.

Borrow: Leveraging Other People's Platforms

Why build an audience from scratch when you can borrow one?

Guest appearances on podcasts, blogs, and video interviews put you in front of a ready-made audience. It's like being the opening act for a famous band.

Tim Ferriss nailed this strategy when launching "The 4-Hour Body." He went on a massive podcast tour, reaching millions of listeners. The result? A New York Times bestseller.

To secure guest spots, offer value, pitch unique angles, and make it easy for the host to say yes.

Buy: Strategic Use of Paid Advertising

Paid ads can amplify your reach, but use them wisely.

The goal? Build your list and provide value. Not just push for immediate sales.

Try a "free + shipping" book offer. You're using ads to get your valuable content into people's hands. It's a relationship starter, not just a sales tactic.

Remember the Nielsen study? Recommendations from people we know are still the most credible form of advertising. Focus on building relationships, and word-of-mouth marketing will follow.

Today's Exercise: Create Your Audience Attraction Playbook Draft

Are you ready to implement the Audience Attraction Playbook? Let's roll up our sleeves and get to work.

Grab a pen and paper. We're about to map out your personalized strategy.

Step 1: Identify Your Primary Capture Method

What's your irresistible lead magnet? A cheat sheet? Mini-course? Free consultation?

Brainstorm five ideas. Pick the one that makes you think, "I'd sign up for that in a heartbeat."

Step 2: Choose Your Strategies

- Boost: How will you amp up your social media game? Maybe it's daily tips on Instagram. Or thought-provoking questions on LinkedIn.

- Build: What evergreen content will you create? A weekly blog post? A monthly podcast episode? A YouTube tutorial series?

- Borrow: Where can you guest star? Find three podcasts, blogs, or YouTube channels in your niche. They're your targets.

Step 3: Outline a Buy Strategy

If you had $100 to spend on ads, how would you use it? Perhaps a Facebook ad promoting your lead magnet? Or a "free + shipping" offer for your book?

Step 4: Craft Your 60-Day Sample Plan

Let's focus on the "Build" strategy, specifically creating a blog to generate evergreen content over eight weeks. Here's a sample 60-day traffic plan:

- Week 1: Research and Planning

- Week 2: Set Up Your Blog

- Week 3: Write Your First Blog Post

- Week 4: Promote Your First Post

- Week 5: Create and Publish Your Second Post

- Week 6: Optimize for SEO

- Week 7: Expand Your Content

- Week 8: Analyze and Adjust

This plan focuses on the "Build" strategy, specifically blogging. It aims to create a strong base of evergreen content in 8 weeks.

Remember, progress over perfection. This is your roadmap to becoming a customer magnet.

Key Takeaways:

- Pull marketing focuses on building relationships, leading to long-term business success.

- The Audience Attraction Playbook consists of five key elements: Capture, Boost, Build, Borrow, and Buy.

- A mix of these strategies creates a solid approach to growing and engaging the audience.

2

The Capture Habit (The Secret to Everything)

In May 2009, Ryan Holiday had an idea. He'd been sharing book recommendations on his website, but what if he turned it into a monthly email instead? A friend warned him it was a bad idea. Who'd want to sign up for that?

Holiday ignored the advice. Five years later, his Reading List Email had grown from 50 friends to 35,000 subscribers worldwide. High school students, Fortune 500 CEOs, NFL coaches, and bestselling authors tuned in for his monthly book picks.

The secret? Consistency, quality, and a laser focus on providing value. Over the years, Holiday sent nearly 100 emails recommending books he genuinely loved. He kept it simple—no frills, just text. And he protected his list fiercely, rarely using it for self-promotion.

This approach paid off in unexpected ways. When Holiday launched his first book, his email list was enough to rock the Amazon charts. He had less than 5,000 subscribers at the time.[2]

Holiday's story illustrates a powerful truth: building an email list is about more than just collecting addresses. It's about creating a community of engaged readers who trust your recommendations and look forward to hearing from you.

In this chapter, we'll explore why email lists are the secret sauce of online business success. We'll break down the strategies that helped

Holiday and others build thriving communities. And we'll show you how to cultivate the habits that turn a simple mailing list into a powerful business asset.

The Magic of Email Lists: Your Secret Weapon for Online Success

Ever wonder how some businesses seem to have a direct line to their customers' hearts (and wallets)? The answer might be sitting in your inbox right now.

Let's talk about email lists. Not the most exciting topic, right? Wrong. Email lists are the unsung heroes of the digital marketing world. They're like that reliable friend who's always there when you need them - steady, dependable, and surprisingly powerful.

Why Your Email List is Your New Best Friend

Reason 1. You're the Boss

Imagine you've built a massive following on social media. Thousands of fans hang on to your every word, and you're on top of the world! Then, one day, poof! The platform changes its algorithm, and your posts vanish into the digital void. Scary, huh?

That's the beauty of an email list. It's yours—all yours. There is no middleman, no algorithm changes, and no disappearing act. When you have someone's email, you have a direct line to their attention. It's like having a key to their digital front door.

Reason 2. Money Talks

Let's get down to brass tacks. Email marketing isn't just practical - it's a money-making machine. You can expect to see $42 in return for every dollar you spend on email marketing. That's not a typo. Forty-two dollars. Try getting that kind of return from your savings account!

Why so lucrative? Simple. Email is personal. It's targeted. It lands right in your customer's personal space, where they're already in a mindset to engage with content. It's like whispering a secret directly into their ear.

Reason 3. Personal Touch

Speaking of personal, let's talk about connection. Social media is like shouting in a crowded room. Email? It's a cozy fireside chat.

When someone gives you their email, they invite you into their world. They're saying, "Hey, I trust you. I want to hear what you have to say." That's powerful stuff. It's an opportunity to build genuine, lasting relationships with your audience.

Reason 4. Numbers Don't Lie

Here's the thing about email - you can measure everything. Open rates, click-through rates, conversions - it's all there in black and white. It's like having a crystal ball that tells you exactly what your audience likes and doesn't like.

This treasure trove of data lets you fine-tune your approach. You can test different subject lines, tweak your content, and optimize your send times. It's like having a superpower that lets you read your customers' minds.

Reason 5. Infinitely Scaleable

Remember Ryan Holiday? He started with just 50 friends on his email list. Five years later? 35,000 subscribers. That's the magic of email lists - they can grow from a tiny seed into a mighty oak.

The best part? Whether you're sending to 100 people or 100,000, the process is pretty much the same. It's scalable. It grows with you. It's like having a business partner that never gets tired and never asks for a raise.

Reason 6. Builds Authority

Want to know a secret? Consistent, valuable emails make you look like a rock star in your field. Every time you pop into someone's inbox with a nugget of wisdom, you're cementing your status as the go-to expert.

Over time, this trust translates into cold, hard cash. When your subscribers see you as the authority, guess who they'll turn to when they need what you're selling? That's right - you.

Reason 7. The Great Traffic Amplifier

Here's the kicker - your email list isn't just powerful on its own. It's like a steroid for all your other marketing efforts.

Got a new blog post? Your email list will drive traffic. Launching a product? Your email list will spread the word. Running a sale? You guessed it - your email list will bring in the customers.

It's the Swiss Army knife of marketing tools. Versatile, reliable, and always there when you need it.

Today's Exercise: Brainstorm Your Capture Ideas

You're convinced, right? Email lists are the bee's knees. But how do you get started? How do you turn this knowledge into action?

Here's a little exercise to kick things off:

1. Write down three reasons why someone would want to join your email list. What can you offer that's truly valuable?

2. Now, brainstorm five ways you could entice people to sign up. A free ebook? A discount code? A weekly tips newsletter?

3. Pick your favorite idea and sketch out a quick plan to implement it. What steps would you need to take?

4. Set a goal. How many subscribers do you want in 3 months? 6 months? A year?

Remember, building an email list isn't about overnight success. It's about consistent effort and providing real value. It's about building relationships, one subscriber at a time.

So, are you ready to harness the power of email marketing? Your future customers are waiting in their inboxes. It's time to say hello.

Key Takeaways:

• Your email list is your most valuable digital asset. It's the only audience you truly own and control. It's immune to algorithm changes and platform shifts.

- Email marketing has the best ROI. It makes $42 for every dollar spent. It enables direct, personal communication with an engaged audience.

- Valuable emails build trust and authority. They turn your list into a powerful tool for driving traffic, launching products, and boosting your marketing.

3

Create an Attractive Lead Magnet (The Dirty Dozen)

A massive wooden horse gleaming in the sunlight outside Troy's impenetrable walls—a gift, the Trojans thought. Little did they know that this "generous offering" would be their downfall.

For ten long years, the Greeks had besieged Troy. No battering ram could breach its defenses. No amount of strength could topple its towers. Then, Odysseus had an idea—a lightbulb moment, if you will.

"What if we could get them to invite us in?"

And so, the Trojan Horse was born—a beautiful, intricately carved wooden horse - large enough to hide a small army inside. The Greeks left it outside Troy's gates and pretended to sail away.

The Trojans, curious and flattered, wheeled the horse inside their city. Greek soldiers poured out of the horse that night, opened the gates, and Troy fell.[3]

You might be thinking, "What's this got to do with my blog?"

Everything.

The Trojan Horse is the original lead magnet. It was attractive, promised value, and got the Greeks exactly where they wanted to be—inside the gates.

Your lead magnets are your modern-day Trojan Horses. They're your ticket into the most valuable real estate in the digital world - your audience's inbox.

But here's the twist: unlike the Greeks, you're not out to conquer. You're offering real value. Your lead magnets are gifts that keep on giving, building trust, and establishing your expertise.

So, are you ready to craft your own Trojan Horse? Let's dive in. We will learn to create irresistible lead magnets. Your audience will be clicking the "Subscribe" button in no time.

The Lead Magnet Trap: Are You Falling For It?

Let's face it. Many bloggers and entrepreneurs are failing when it comes to lead magnets. They're ignoring them, making dull freebies, or getting too complex.

The Overlookers

Some folks are so focused on pumping out content that they forget about lead magnets altogether. It's like throwing a party and forgetting to send out invitations. A few people might stumble in, but you're missing out on the actual crowd.

The Generic Generators

Then, some slap together a quick, one-size-fits-all freebie. "How to cook a tasty dinner" might sound good, but it's about as exciting as plain toast. Your audience is hungry for a gourmet meal, not leftover crumbs.

The Perfectionists

On the flip side, we've got the perfectionists. They're crafting the Mona Lisa of lead magnets, pouring hours into every detail. Admirable, but are they missing the forest for the trees?

Why These Approaches Fall Flat

Generic doesn't cut it anymore. Your lead magnet must be a lighthouse, not another wave in a sea of content. Low-value freebies? They're like cheap party favors - forgotten as soon as received. And those overly complex creations? They might impress, but they can overwhelm your audience and drain your time.

So, what's the secret sauce?

Keep It Simple, Make It Valuable

Think of your lead magnet as a sample platter. It should give your audience a taste of your expertise and leave them satisfied but still hungry for more. How?

Focus on solving one specific problem. Your audience has pain points - be the aspirin.

Mix it up. Some people love to read; others prefer to listen or watch. Cater to different learning styles.

Aim for quick wins. Give your audience something they can implement right away. Nothing builds trust like results.

Remember, your lead magnet is a handshake, not a bear hug. It's an introduction, a teaser of the value you can provide. Make it count, make it simple, and watch your email list grow.

Ready to craft lead magnets that actually work? Let's dive into the Dirty Dozen - twelve lead magnet ideas that'll have your audience clicking "subscribe" faster than you can say "email list."

The Dirty Dozen: 12 Lead Magnets to Supercharge Your Email List

Before we cover the dirty dozen, it's important to note that you do not need to create all twelve lead magnet ideas to succeed. Pick a few that you like and make something valuable. Remember, we are creating these to capture traffic on an email list. Later in the book, you'll learn fourteen traffic methods to supercharge your list-building efforts.

1. Checklist or Resource List

Ever feel overwhelmed by a long blog post? Your readers do, too. That's where checklists come in. Take that meaty content and boil it down to its essence. A simple, actionable checklist can be a game-changer.

Think of it as a map for your readers. It guides them through the journey you've outlined in your content. No more getting lost in the details. Just clear, step-by-step directions to success.

2. Audio Transcript

Got a podcast or video series? Don't let that content go to waste. Some folks love to listen, others prefer to read. Why not cater to both? Give your audience options. Some learn by listening, others by reading. Cater to both with audio transcripts.

3. PDF Blog Post

Your blog post is a hit. But what if your readers want to save it for later? Enter the PDF version. It's like turning your post into a mini-ebook.

Think of it as a takeaway menu from your favorite restaurant. Your readers can enjoy your content on their own time and terms. No internet? No problem. They've got your wisdom right at their fingertips.

4. Tip Sheet

Who doesn't love a good tip? Compile your best advice into a handy tip sheet. It's quick to create and even quicker for your readers to consume. The best tip sheets are like a Swiss Army knife for your readers—compact, versatile, and very useful.

5. Useful Worksheet

Help your readers put your advice into action. A worksheet turns passive reading into active doing. It's where the rubber meets the road. Picture it as a personal trainer for your audience's goals. It guides them through the process and keeps them accountable. No more "I'll do it later" excuses.

6. Report or Case Study

Show your readers what success looks like. A short report on industry trends or a case study of a successful client can be powerful. Case studies are your success stories in action. They show, not tell, the value you bring. It's proof that your methods work.

7. Excel File or Spreadsheet

Got a knack for numbers? Share the wealth. A pre-made spreadsheet can be a lifesaver for your audience. It's like a calculator on steroids. It does the heavy lifting so your audience can focus on the results. From budgeting to project planning, the possibilities are endless.

8. Example Template

Why start from scratch when you can give your readers a head start? Templates save time and reduce overwhelm. Templates are the starting blocks for success. They give your audience a head start on their journey. Who wouldn't want that?

9. Manual or Starter Guide

Remember the frustration of assembling furniture without instructions? Don't let your readers feel that way about your topic. A starter guide is like that quick-start manual. It helps your readers achieve early wins and build momentum—no PhD required.

10. Audio File

Sometimes, your audience wants to learn on the go. That's where audio shines. A short, valuable lesson can make a long commute fly by. Audio content is intimate. It's like whispering advice directly into your audience's ears.

11. Instructional Video

Some concepts are more accessible to grasp when you see them in action. That's where video comes in handy. Think of it as show-and-tell for adults. It engages multiple senses and makes learning more immersive. Plus, who doesn't love a good tutorial?

12. Learning Challenge or Free Course

Want to really engage your audience? Challenge them. A multi-day challenge or mini-course can be a powerful tool. A well-crafted learning challenge is like a fitness program for the mind. It builds skills and confidence through consistent, incremental progress.

There you have it - the Dirty Dozen. Twelve lead magnet ideas to attract, engage, and grow your audience. Which one will you try first?

Today's Exercise: Create Your Lead Magnet

It's time to put theory into practice. We're going to create a lead magnet that'll have your audience hitting that subscribe button faster than you can say "email list." Ready? Let's dive in!

Step 1: Pick Your Poison

Look at the Dirty Dozen we just covered. Which one speaks to you? Which one would your audience love? Choose one. Don't overthink it. You can always try others later.

Step 2: Brainstorm Bonanza

Have you got your lead magnet type? Great. Now, what's your niche all about? Jot down 3-5 topics your audience is dying to know more about. What keeps them up at night? What problem can you solve?

Step 3: Outline Like a Pro

It's time to structure your lead magnet. If you chose a checklist, what are the key steps? For a tip sheet, what are your top 10 nuggets of wisdom? Sketch it out. Remember, we're aiming for value, not War and Peace.

Step 4: Create, Don't Procrastinate

Here's where the rubber meets the road. Set a timer for 2-3 hours. Yes, you read that right. We're not aiming for perfection; we're aiming for done. Create a simple version of your lead magnet. Use tools you're comfortable with. Canva is for design, Google Docs is for writing, and whatever works.

So, what are you waiting for? Your audience is out there, hungry for the value you're about to provide. Get creating!

Key Takeaways:

- The simplest solution is often the best when creating lead magnets. Focus on providing quick wins and clear value to your audience.

- Offer different lead magnets. This will cater to your audience's varied learning styles and preferences.

- Create and test new lead magnets. Find what your audience likes best to drive email sign-ups.

4

The Perfect 5-Point Landing Page

I t's 1853, and the Big Apple is abuzz with innovation. Inventors from around the world showcase their latest marvels. But one man's display stands out.

Elisha Otis steps onto a platform high above the crowd. Gasps echo through the hall. What's he doing up there?

With a dramatic flourish, Otis raises his hand. "All safe, gentlemen!" he declares. In an instant, an assistant cuts the only rope holding the platform. Hearts skip a beat. Will Otis plummet to his doom?

But he doesn't fall. The platform jolts, then stops. Otis's revolutionary safety brake has just saved his life - and changed the world.

This wasn't just any demonstration. It was the world's first elevator pitch. In less than a minute, Otis conveyed the value of his invention. There were no long-winded explanations or complicated jargon. Just a clear, impactful message that anyone could understand.

The result? Orders poured in. Elevators went from death traps to must-have amenities. Suddenly, buildings could reach for the sky. The modern city skyline was born.[4]

What made Otis's pitch so effective? It was simple. It was visual. It solved a real problem. And it packed a punch.

Sound familiar? These are the exact same principles that make a great landing page. Just like Otis's elevator, your landing page needs to quickly convey value, solve a problem, and make an impact.

Ready to create your own show-stopping pitch? Let's dive in and learn how to craft the perfect 5-point landing page. It might not revolutionize architecture, but it could certainly revolutionize your business.

The Landing Page Trap

Ever visited a website and felt like you've stumbled into a digital jungle? You're not alone. Most folks treat their landing pages like an all-you-can-eat buffet of information. They pile on paragraphs, sprinkle in some stock photos, and top it off with a generic "Learn More" button. Oh, and don't forget the side dishes - social media links, navigation menus, and popups galore!

But here's the kicker: this approach is about as effective as trying to catch fish with a tennis racket. Why? Let's break it down.

First, information overload is real. When visitors are bombarded with too much content, their brains short-circuit. They freeze up, unsure where to look or what to do next. It's like trying to drink from a fire hose—overwhelming and ultimately ineffective.

Generic headlines and calls to action? They're about as inspiring as lukewarm coffee. In a world where we're constantly bombarded with messages, bland doesn't cut it. Your visitors need a reason to care, and "Click Here" just doesn't light that fire.

And those distractions? Each link, each button, and each shiny object is a potential exit route. It's like setting up a maze when you want your visitors to follow a straight path. Every distraction lowers your conversion rate. It sends potential customers down rabbit holes instead of to your desired action.

So, what's the secret sauce? Think minimalist chic, not information hoarder.

Your landing page should be a laser-focused machine. Every element should point towards a single goal. It's about clarity, not clutter—simplicity, not sensory overload.

Craft content that speaks directly to your visitor's needs and desires. Make them feel seen, understood, and offered a solution they can't resist. Your words should be a magnet, not a megaphone.

And those distractions? Show them the door. Guide your visitors gently but firmly towards the action you want them to take. No detours, no distractions, just a clear path to conversion.

Remember, in the world of landing pages, less isn't just more - it's money in the bank. Ready to turn your landing page from a cluttered mess into a conversion powerhouse? Let's dive into the nitty-gritty of how to make it happen.

The 5-Point Landing Page Blueprint

Ready to turn your landing page into a conversion machine? Let's break down the five essential elements that'll make your page irresistible.

1. Craft a Catchy Headline

Your headline is your first impression. Make it count! You've got three secret weapons in your headline arsenal:

- Curiosity-based: Pique their interest. "The Secret Question You Must Ask Before Starting Your Business"

- Pain-focused: Address their struggles. "Tired of Feeling Stuck in Your Career?"

- Benefit-driven: Show them what they'll gain. "Free Ebook: Get the Clarity You Deserve in Just 5 Days"

Choose the style that best suits your offer. Remember, a great headline is like a newspaper's front-page story—it grabs attention and makes people want to read more.

2. Create Productized Images

Even if your product is digital, make it look tangible. Our brains love concrete, physical things. If it looks real, we value it more. Tools like Canva let you display your digital product on phones, laptops, or tablets.

As one digital marketing expert says, "A picture is worth a thousand words, but a productized image is worth a thousand clicks."

3. Write Compelling Bullet Points

Bullet points are your chance to shine. Use these three types:

- How-to: "How to finally rid yourself of analysis paralysis so you can take massive action."

- List: "4 influence igniters that can explode your platform growth in just 90 days."

- Benefit: "The entrepreneurial opportunity filter scorecard that helps you make good decisions in 5 minutes or less."

Sprinkle-in-time modifiers ("in 90 days") and speed modifiers ("in 5 minutes or less") to amp up the excitement. Good bullet points are like a movie trailer. They excite and leave the audience wanting more.

4. Design a Clear Call-to-Action (CTA)

Your CTA is where the magic happens. Make it specific and action-oriented.

Instead of boring old "Subscribe," try:

- "Yes, Send Me the Action Guide!"

- "Download Now"

- "Get Instant Access"

Remember, your call-to-action is the gateway between your visitor and your offer. Make it impossible to resist.

5. Apply the No-Link Rule

Here's a counterintuitive tip: Remove all navigation menus, contextual links, and distractions—yep, all of them.

Why? Each link is an exit route. You want your visitors focused on one thing and one thing only—your offer.

Think of it this way: a landing page with no external links is like a sales pitch without interruptions - it keeps the focus entirely on your offer.

There you have it – the five-point blueprint for a landing page that converts. Ready to put it into action? Let's move on to a practical exercise to help you implement these strategies.

Today's Exercise: Create Your Perfect Landing Page

It's time to roll up your sleeves and create your own high-converting landing page. Don't worry—we'll take it step by step.

Step 1: Pick Your Star Player

What's the one thing you want to promote? It could be an ebook, a webinar, a free consultation, or any other lead magnet. Choose something you're excited about – your enthusiasm will shine through in your copy.

Step 2: Headline Brainstorm

Now, let's craft three attention-grabbing headlines:

- Curiosity-based: What's the most intriguing aspect of your offer? Tease it here.

- Pain-focused: What problem does your audience desperately want to solve?

- Benefit-driven: What's the biggest gain your offer provides?

Write at least one of each type. Don't worry about perfection – we're brainstorming here!

Step 3: Picture Perfect

Time to make your offer look irresistible. Head over to Canva. Create an image that makes your digital offer look tangible and valuable. Remember, we eat with our eyes first!

Step 4: Bullet Point Bonanza

Craft 3-5 killer bullet points. Mix and match these types:

- How-to: "How to [achieve the desired outcome] so you can [enjoy benefit]."

- List: "[Number] ways to [achieve the desired outcome] in [timeframe]."

- Benefit: "The [your offer] that [provides specific benefit] in [timeframe]."

Don't forget to sprinkle in those time and speed modifiers!

Step 5: Call-to-Action Creation

Design a CTA button that screams, "Click me!" Make it specific to your offer and action-oriented. "Yes, I Want [Specific Benefit]!" often works well.

Step 6: Declutter and Focus

Look at your current landing page. Ruthlessly remove any links, menus, or elements that don't directly contribute to your conversion goal. Be brave – less is more!

Step 7: Test and Tweak

Share your new landing page with a small audience. This could be your email list, social media followers, or even friends and family. Track how many people visit and how many convert.

Don't be discouraged if your first attempt isn't perfect. Landing page optimization is an ongoing process. Analyze your results, make adjustments, and test again.

Remember, every master was once a beginner. The key is to start, learn, and keep improving. Now, go forth and create a landing page that converts!

Key Takeaways:

- A well-designed landing page follows a 5-point checklist: catchy headline, productized image, compelling bullet points, clear CTA, and no distracting links.

- Simplicity and focus are crucial for high-converting landing pages – remove distractions and guide visitors toward a single action.

- Continuously test and refine your landing pages to improve conversion rates and grow your audience more effectively.

5

The Lead Magnet Launch Pad (Skyrocket Your Email List)

I n November 2011, I published a blog post on my fairly new blog, Simple Life Habits. The topic of the blog post? The power of taking real breaks to stay motivated and creative throughout the day. Little did I know that this simple post would lead to a pivotal moment in my blogging journey—and a harsh lesson in missed opportunities.

A few days after publishing, I checked my Google Analytics account and was shocked. My traffic had increased tenfold overnight, and thousands of views were pouring in daily, but I had no idea where they came from. I found something spectacular after some digging. A writer at Lifehacker, a popular site, had featured my blog post and linked to my site.

It was a blogger's dream come true. Or so I thought.

You see, in my excitement to create content, I had made a colossal mistake. I hadn't set up any way for these thousands of new visitors to join an email list. A flood of potential long-term readers visited my site for several days, only to leave without a trace. Had I had a lead magnet and a landing page in place, I could have easily captured hundreds, if not thousands, of new email subscribers.

This experience taught me a valuable lesson: traffic alone doesn't build a business. It's the leads on an email list that can nurture and grow your audience for years to come. We're dedicating this chapter to maximizing your lead magnet exposure for rapid list growth.

We'll explore strategies for placing your lead magnet on multiple platforms. You'll learn how to transform every piece of content—a blog post, podcast episode, or social media update—into an opportunity to grow your email list.

Remember, an email list is more than just a collection of addresses. It's a direct line to your most engaged audience. It's a way to build relationships. And, it's the foundation of a sustainable online business. By the end of this chapter, you'll have the tools and strategies to turn casual visitors into loyal subscribers. This will set the stage for long-term success in your digital efforts.

Let's dive in and ensure you never miss an opportunity to grow your most valuable asset—your email list.

Common Pitfalls in List Building

Each visitor to your site is a potential gold mine. But are you treating them that way? Most folks underestimate the value of a single visitor. They think, "Oh, it's just one person." But what if that one person becomes your biggest fan? Your most vocal advocate? Your next big client?

And let's talk about those unexpected traffic surges. They're like winning the lottery, right? Wrong. If you're not prepared, they're more like finding a briefcase full of cash... and having no pockets—all that potential, gone in a flash.

Why Traditional Approaches Fall Short

You've got a killer website. Great content. Steady traffic. So why isn't your business growing like wildfire?

Here's the harsh truth: one-time visitors are like speed dating. You get a quick hello, maybe a bit of small talk, and then... poof! They're gone. How are you supposed to build a relationship with someone who's already out the door?

Think about it. How many times have you stumbled across a fantastic blog post, thought, "Wow, I need to remember this site!" and never returned? That's the reality for most of your visitors. Without a way to stay connected, you're losing opportunities for long-term engagement faster than a melting ice cream cone on a hot summer day.

But here's the real kicker: even if you're getting tons of traffic, if you can't convert that into a growing email list, you're leaving money on the table. It's like having a store full of window shoppers but no way to tell them about your sales. All that potential business growth? Slipping through your fingers like sand.

So, what's the solution? How do we turn these pitfalls into stepping stones? Stick around. We're about to flip the script on traditional list building and show you how to turn every piece of content into a lead-generating powerhouse.

The "Everywhere All At Once" Strategy

Ever wished you could clone yourself? To be in multiple places at once, chatting up potential subscribers left and right? With the

"Everywhere All At Once" strategy, your lead magnet becomes your digital doppelganger.

What's the big idea? Simple. We're taking your lead magnet and sharing it across every platform you're on. Blog? Check. Social media? You bet. Podcast? Absolutely. It's like turning your lead magnet into a pop star on a world tour – showing up wherever your audience hangs out.

But why go through all this trouble?

Picture this: You're fishing. One rod, one spot. You can only catch one fish at a time. Our method? It's like casting a net across the entire lake. More lines in the water mean more fish on the hook. In this case, more eyeballs on your lead magnet mean more names on your list.

And here's the kicker – it's not just about quantity. You're catching people at various stages of their journey by popping up in different contexts. Someone who ignores your tweet might devour your blog post. A podcast listener who skips the show notes might click on your YouTube description. You're creating multiple touchpoints and multiple chances to convert.

The beauty of this strategy? It turns every piece of content you create into a potential list-building machine. You're not just creating content; you're creating opportunities. Opportunities to connect, to provide value, and yes, to grow that all-important email list.

Ready to become omnipresent in your niche? Let's explain exactly how to tailor your lead magnet for each platform. Your audience won't know what hit them – in the best way possible.

How to Skyrocket Your Email List

A smart approach to email list building is to always have a call to action with every piece of content you create. When you use the traffic playbooks later in this book, add a link to your landing page and freebie. This will help you grow your email list with all that traffic. Here's how to optimize your email list building as you create content:

Social Media Posts

Your social media bio is prime real estate for lead magnet promotion. Don't waste it on generic information. Instead, use it to showcase your most valuable free resource. Craft a compelling one-liner that highlights the benefit of your lead magnet. For example, "Get my free guide: Triple Your Productivity in 7 Days." This instantly communicates value to your followers.

Pro tip: Use a tool like Linktree to create a single link in your bio that leads to multiple resources, including your lead magnet. This way, you're not limited to promoting just one thing.

Private Facebook Group

Facebook groups are goldmines for list building if you use them strategically. When someone requests to join your group, Facebook allows you to ask them up to three questions. Use this feature to your advantage!

One of your questions could be: "Would you like access to [Your Lead Magnet]? If yes, please enter your email address." This approach is brilliant. It captures emails from your most engaged audience: those who joined your community.

You can even create a pinned post highlighting your lead magnet in your group. Update it regularly to keep it fresh and engaging. Remember, subtlety is key in groups. Provide value first, and let your lead magnet be the cherry on top.

Blog Posts

Blog posts are perfect for implementing the content upgrade strategy. A content upgrade is a lead magnet specific to a particular blog post. It provides additional value related to the post's topic.

For example, if your post is "10 Ways to Improve Your Public Speaking," your content upgrade could be a "Public Speaking Confidence Checklist." This relevance makes it irresistible to readers already engaged with your content.

As for placement, the 25% mark is ideal for your first CTA. Why? Because readers who've made it this far are engaged with your content. They're primed to want more. Use a colorful box or a different font to make your CTA stand out.

Don't forget to include another CTA at the end of your post. Readers who've made it to the end are your most engaged audience. They're hungry for more. Give them what they want!

Podcast Episodes

Your podcast intro and outro are prime real estate for lead magnet promotion. In your intro, tease your lead magnet. "Stay tuned till the end to learn how you can get my free guide on [topic]." This creates anticipation and gives listeners a reason to stick around.

In your outro, deliver on that promise. Provide clear instructions on how to get the lead magnet. "To get your free copy of [Lead Magnet], simply visit [easy-to-remember URL]." Repeat the URL twice to ensure listeners catch it.

Don't neglect your show notes! Many podcast listeners check show notes for links and resources mentioned in the episode. Include a clear, compelling CTA and link to your lead magnet here. You could even create a custom graphic for your lead magnet to make it more visually appealing.

YouTube Videos

YouTube offers multiple opportunities for lead magnet promotion. Start by mentioning your lead magnet at the beginning of your video. "Before we dive in, don't forget to grab my free guide on [topic]. The link is in the description below."

At the end of your video, reinforce the offer. "If you found this video helpful, you'll love my comprehensive guide on [topic]. Click the link below to get your free copy." This reminds viewers of the value you're offering.

The video description is crucial for conversions. Place your lead magnet link near the top, ideally in the first couple of lines. YouTube truncates descriptions, so don't bury your link.

Use YouTube cards and end screens to promote your lead magnet. These clickable elements can lead directly to your landing page. They're like signposts guiding viewers to your valuable free resource.

Medium Articles

Medium offers a unique platform for content creators but requires a nuanced approach to lead magnet promotion. The key is to adapt your strategy based on whether you publish on your personal account or in a publication.

For personal posts, you have more freedom. Incorporate a clear call-to-action for your lead magnet within the article itself. Use Medium's built-in features like pull quotes or section breaks to make your CTA stand out. For example, after a particularly insightful paragraph, you might add: "Want to dive deeper into this topic? Get my free guide on [topic] that expands on these ideas."

Publication posts often have stricter guidelines. Some may not allow direct promotion within the article. In these cases, focus on crafting an irresistible author bio. This is your secret weapon on Medium.

Pinterest Pins

Pinterest is a visual search engine perfect for lead magnet promotion. You can use two main strategies here: direct pins and blog post-integration.

Direct pins are standalone images created specifically to promote your lead magnet. These should be visually striking and include a clear CTA. Use bold text overlays like "Free Guide: 10 Easy Meal Prep Recipes" or "Download Now: Home Organization Checklist."

Blog post-integration means making pins for your blog content. Each pin must mention your related lead magnet. This strategy works well because it provides value upfront (the blog content) while teasing even more value (the lead magnet).

Guest Blog Posts

Guest blogging is a powerful way to get your lead magnet in front of new audiences. The key is to leverage your author bio effectively.

Your author bio is more than an afterthought—it's your chance to shine. Craft it to highlight your expertise and seamlessly introduce your lead magnet. For example: "Sarah Johnson is a digital marketing expert who has helped over 100 businesses boost their online presence. Get her free 'SEO Quickstart Guide' at sarahjohnson.com/seo-guide."

Guest Podcast Interviews

Podcast interviews pose a challenge. You must promote your lead magnet verbally. That's where memorable domain names help.

Craft a domain name that's short, catchy, and easy to spell. Instead of "yourname.com/free-marketing-guide," try something like "quickmarketingtips.com" or "marketingboostguide.com." Practice saying it out loud to ensure it rolls off the tongue easily.

The best time to share your lead magnet is at the end of the interview when the host asks, "Where can listeners best connect with you?"

Remember, the goal is to come across as helpful, not pushy. Your lead magnet should feel like a natural extension of the value you're providing in the interview.

Guest Video Interviews

The strategy for guest video interviews is very similar to podcasting. At the end of the interview, the host often asks where people can connect with you. This is your opportunity to share your free resource and the link where they can get it.

Guest Email Swaps

The primary goal of the guest email swap strategy (as you'll learn later in the book) is to build your email list from someone else's email list. In other words, they will send one to three emails to their list about your lead magnet. Everyone interested will click on the link and join your email list. Why would partners agree to this? Because you'll be returning the favor by sending their lead magnet to your email list.

Paid Traffic Campaigns

While organic strategies are great, sometimes you need to boost your list growth with paid traffic. Facebook ads, in particular, can be highly effective for lead magnet promotion.

The power of Facebook ads lies in their targeting capabilities. You can narrow down your audience based on demographics, interests, behaviors, and even life events. This precision ensures your lead magnet gets in front of the right eyes.

The ad itself is simple. You show an image of the lead magnet and some reasons why they should grab it, with a link to your landing page. You'll learn more about this strategy later in the book.

There you have it—several ways to skyrocket your email list. If you adopt this practice, you'll have hundreds of ways new people can get on your email list over time.

Today's Exercise: Craft Your Lead Magnet's Irresistible Pitch

Ready to turn your lead magnet into an irresistible offer? Let's craft a pitch that'll have your audience clicking faster than you can say, "free download!"

Imagine you're at a party, and someone asks what you do. You've got two sentences to make them want your lead magnet so badly that they're ready to trade their dessert for it. Here's what you need to pack into those sentences:

- What's your lead magnet? A guide? A checklist? A video series?

- What's the big, juicy benefit? How will it change their life?

- What should they do right now to get it?

Got your first draft? Great! Now, let's make it pop. Swap out boring words for vibrant ones. "Get" becomes "Unlock". "Learn" transforms into "Master". Make every word earn its place!

Your pitch might go: "Unlock the secrets of productivity with our free '5-Minute Focus Finder' guide. Click the link in our bio to transform your workday and reclaim hours of lost time!"

It tells you what it is (a guide), the benefits (effortless productivity and reclaimed time), and what to do (click the link).

Now it's your turn. Craft a pitch that makes your lead magnet sound like the best thing since sliced bread. Because to your ideal audience, it just might be!

Key Takeaways:

- Maximize every touchpoint. Turn each content piece into a list-building chance by placing your lead magnet CTAs.

- Diversify your approach: Utilize a mix of owned, earned, and paid media to create multiple pathways for audience members to join your list.

- Prepare for success: Always have a lead capture system. It will turn one-time visitors into long-term subscribers. It will capitalize on traffic surges.

6

Choose Your Own Traffic Adventure

Remember those Choose Your Own Adventure books from middle school? You'd flip to page 106 to walk through door number one or page 135 for door number two. Each choice led you down a different path, making you the hero of your own story.

That's exactly how I want you to approach the traffic playbooks in the following chapters. This book is not designed for you to tackle all of the 14 traffic methods at a time. Instead, pick one and commit to it for 60 days. It's your adventure, your choice.

Why focus on just one method? Imagine trying to read all those adventure books at once. Confusing, right? The same goes for traffic generation. By zeroing in on a single strategy, you'll master it faster and see real results.

So, are you ready to choose your own traffic adventure? Let's dive in and find the perfect path to building your audience.

Common Mistakes in Traffic Generation

Ever feel like you're running on a hamster wheel trying to grow your audience? You're not alone. Many people fall into the trap of juggling multiple traffic strategies at once. They post on every social platform, write blog posts and guest blogs, and try to master SEO. It's exhausting and, frankly, ineffective.

The problem? Lack of focus and consistency. When you spread yourself thin, you can't give any one method the attention it deserves. It's like trying to learn five languages at once - you might pick up a few words here and there, but you won't become fluent in any of them.

The Power of Concentrated Effort

Here's a radical idea: what if you focused on just one traffic method for 60 days? Sounds simple, right? But it's a game-changer.

Why 60 days? It's long enough to see actual results but short enough to stay motivated. By dedicating yourself to a single strategy, you'll dive deep, learn the nuances, and see progress. It's like choosing and practicing one language daily - suddenly, you're having conversations!

This focused approach leads to mastery. You'll become an expert in your chosen method, understanding what works and what doesn't. And with expertise comes better results. You're not just throwing spaghetti at the wall anymore - you're cooking a gourmet meal.

Four Main Traffic Methods

Let's go ahead and break down your options. Think of these as the main chapters in your traffic adventure:

- Boost: This is all about social media traffic. It's fast-paced and constantly changing, and it can be a goldmine if you know how to navigate it.

- Build: Here's where search engine optimization (SEO) comes in. It's about creating content that ranks well on search engines through blogging, podcasting, or YouTube videos.

- Borrow: This strategy leverages other people's audiences. Guest blogging, being featured in newsletters, or appearing on podcasts are all ways to expand your reach through partnerships.

- Buy: While not always necessary, paid advertising can be a powerful tool when used wisely.

Remember, you don't need to master all of these. Your adventure, your choice. Which path will you choose?

Guidelines for Choosing and Implementing Your Traffic Adventure

Ready to start your journey? Here's your roadmap:

1. Assess Your Strengths and Resources

Take a good, hard look at yourself. What are you good at? What do you enjoy doing? Do you have a knack for writing, or are you a natural on camera? How much time can you realistically dedicate to this?

Choosing a traffic method is like selecting the right tool from a toolbox - pick the one that fits the job. If you're a wordsmith, blogging may be your path. If you're charismatic on video, YouTube could be your goldmine.

2. Identify Your Target Audience's Preferred Platforms

Where do your ideal customers hang out online? Are they scrolling through Instagram, or are they more likely to search on Google? Do they prefer reading blog posts or watching videos?

Remember the old marketing proverb: "Fish where the fish are." There's no point in mastering Twitter if your audience is all on LinkedIn.

3. Select One Traffic Playbook

Now, match your strengths with your audience's preferences. Choose ONE method that aligns with both—yes, just one—and commit to it for 60 days.

Your traffic strategy is like a garden. Plant one seed, nurture it daily, and watch it grow into a flourishing source of visitors. Trying to plant the whole packet at once will result in a mess, not a garden.

4. Create a 60-Day Action Plan

Break your chosen method down into bite-sized daily tasks. What do you need to do each day to make this work? Be specific and realistic.

Antoine de Saint-Exupéry said best: "A goal without a plan is just a wish." Don't just wish for more traffic - plan for it.

5. Implement and Track Progress

Now comes the hard part—actually doing the work. Stick to your plan, be consistent, and, most importantly, track your results.

Tracking your traffic is like using a GPS on a road trip. It shows you if you're on the right path or need to make adjustments. Are your numbers going up? Great! Not seeing results? Time to tweak your approach.

Remember, this is your adventure. You're in control. Ready to choose your path?

Today's Exercise: Your One-Day Traffic Method Selection

Let's put theory into practice. Today, you will choose your traffic adventure and map out your journey. Grab a pen and paper or open up a new document. Ready? Let's go!

1. List Your Top Three Skills

What are you great at? Maybe you're a wizard with words, a video virtuoso, or a social media savant. Jot down your top three skills related to content creation or marketing. Be honest with yourself - what truly comes naturally to you?

2. Identify Your Audience's Favorite Platforms

Where does your target audience hang out online? Think about the three online platforms they use most. Are they LinkedIn professionals? Instagram scrollers? YouTube watchers? If you're not sure, it's time for some quick research. Check out industry reports or ask a few of your ideal customers.

3. Choose Your Traffic Playbook

Now, match your skills with your audience's preferred platforms. Which traffic method sits at the intersection of what you're good at and where your audience is? That's your winner. Remember, you're committing to this for 60 days, so choose something you'll enjoy.

4. Outline Your 60-Day Plan

Time to get specific. Break your chosen method down into actionable steps. What will you do daily or weekly to make this work? Here's what to include:

- Daily or weekly action items: Be specific. "Post on Instagram" isn't enough. How about "Create and post one carousel infographic on Instagram every Tuesday and Thursday"?

- Key metrics to track: How will you measure success? Followers, engagement rate, website traffic?

- Resources needed: What tools will you use? How much time will you dedicate each day? Do you need to collaborate with anyone?

5. Get Feedback

Don't keep your plan to yourself. Share it with a colleague, mentor, or even a fellow entrepreneur. Ask for their honest feedback. Are you being realistic? Have you overlooked anything?

Remember, this exercise isn't about creating the perfect plan. It's about getting started. You can (and should) adjust as you go. The important thing is to choose your adventure and take that first step.

So, what's it going to be? Which traffic method will you master in the next 60 days?

Key Takeaways:

- Focusing on one traffic method for 60 days is more effective than trying multiple strategies simultaneously.

- Choose a traffic playbook that aligns with your strengths and where your target audience is most active online.

- To build your audience, you must consistently use and track your chosen method.

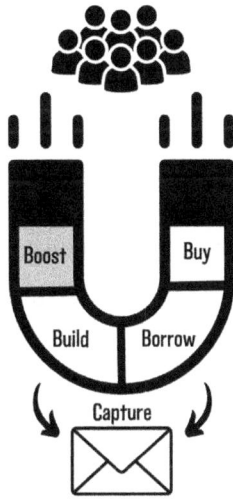

The Boost Method
(Social Traffic)

7

The Daily Post Traffic Playbook

I n the bustling world of social media, one name stands out as a testament to the power of consistency and value-driven content: Justin Welsh. Starting from scratch, Welsh built a thriving business. He gained a devoted following by posting one valuable LinkedIn post daily. It was a simple yet powerful strategy.

Like many others, Welsh's journey began with a desire to share his expertise and build a personal brand. But, unlike those who posted sporadically or self-promoted, he committed to a daily ritual. He crafted thoughtful, engaging posts. Each day, without fail, Welsh would show up in his followers' feeds with insights, tips, and relatable stories.

His approach wasn't about constant self-promotion or chasing viral moments. Instead, he focused on providing genuine value to his audience. Some days, he'd share practical advice on building a business. On other days, he'd offer a contrarian view on a popular topic, sparking lively discussions. And sometimes, he'd share a personal story that resonated with his followers' experiences.

The results were remarkable. Over time, Welsh's audience grew from a handful of connections to tens of thousands of engaged followers. His daily posts became a must-read for entrepreneurs and professionals. They sought insights and inspiration. More importantly, this presence led to business success. Welsh built a seven-figure business mainly through relationships from his daily LinkedIn activity.[5]

Welsh's story illustrates a fundamental truth about social media success: it's not about grand gestures or viral hits. It's about showing up daily with content that adds value to your audience's lives. It's about building trust and relationships through consistent, thoughtful engagement.

This approach isn't limited to LinkedIn or any particular industry. Those who post valuable content regularly build engaged audiences. They reap the rewards in their businesses and careers.

The power of the daily post strategy lies in its simplicity and compound effect. Each post might seem small. But, they build a strong body of work over time. It will establish your expertise, grow your audience, and open doors to opportunities.

In this chapter, we'll explore how you can implement your own daily post strategy, regardless of your chosen platform or niche. We'll explore four types of engaging posts. They can form the backbone of your content strategy. We'll also give tips for crafting compelling content every day.

Remember, the goal isn't perfection or virality. It's about consistency, value, and genuine connection with your audience. By committing to this daily practice, you, too, can build a loyal following and create opportunities for your business or career to thrive.

So, let's roll up our sleeves and discover how you can harness the power of the daily post to build your audience and achieve your goals.

What Most People Do Wrong on Social Media

Most people approach social media with a haphazard strategy if any at all. They post when inspiration strikes, often leading to irregular and infrequent updates. Some fall into the trap of self-promotion. They turn their feeds into digital billboards, not spaces for engagement. Others lack a strategy. They post whatever comes to mind, ignoring their audience's needs.

Many users also make the mistake of chasing viral moments. They try to copy trending content or create flashy, attention-grabbing posts. They don't consider if they provide real value to their followers. This method may get a few likes or shares. But, it rarely leads to lasting engagement or business success.

Why That Doesn't Work

These standard approaches fail for several reasons. First, social media algorithms favor accounts that post consistently and generate regular engagement. Sporadic posting makes gaining traction and visibility in followers' feeds difficult.

Self-promotion is sometimes needed. But, it hurts social media's goal of building relationships. Followers quickly tune out accounts constantly selling, leading to decreased engagement and reach.

A lack of strategy leads to inconsistent messaging, which makes it hard for followers to know what to expect from an account. This inconsistency can erode trust and make it difficult to build a loyal audience.

Chasing viral moments might provide a temporary boost, but it's not a sustainable strategy. Constantly changing your voice or content style to fit the latest trend can also damage your brand.

The Daily Post Strategy: An Overview

Instead of these ineffective approaches, I suggest adopting a daily post strategy. This involves committing to sharing valuable content every single day on your chosen platform(s). The key is consistency and focusing on providing genuine value to your audience.

The daily post strategy isn't about promotion or sales. It's about building relationships, establishing trust, and being a valuable resource in your niche. By posting daily content that educates, entertains, empowers, or empathizes with your audience, you build a strong foundation for lasting engagement and success.

Steps to Implement the Daily Post Strategy

1. Choose Your Platform

The first step in implementing your daily post strategy is selecting the right platforms. While it might be tempting to be everywhere at once, it's more effective to focus your efforts where your target audience spends their time.

Research where your ideal followers are most active. Are they professionals scrolling through LinkedIn? Creatives browsing Instagram? Gen Z users on TikTok? Choose one or two platforms that align best with your audience and content style.

Remember, quality trumps quantity. Having a strong, consistent presence on one platform is better than a weak, sporadic presence on many.

2. Write Your Posts Once a Week

Consistency doesn't have to mean daily stress. One of the most effective ways to maintain your daily posting strategy is to batch your content creation. Set aside one hour each week to write your seven social media posts for the upcoming week. This approach lets you focus your creativity, stay consistent, and save time to engage with your audience.

Choose a time when you're typically at your most creative and energetic. For some, this might be Sunday evening as they prepare for the week ahead. For others, it could be Wednesday afternoon when they need a break from other tasks. The key is to find a time that works for you and stick to it.

During this focused hour, aim to write seven helpful social media posts. Remember, these can be short - shorter posts often perform better on most platforms. Aim for posts that can be read in under a minute but provide real value to your audience.

It's important to note that graphics, while sometimes helpful, are optional for some posts. Many successful social media personalities build large followings with text-only posts. The power is in the words you write and the value you provide, not in flashy visuals.

The good news is that you don't need to reinvent the wheel for every post. You can use and reuse proven social media templates. These templates provide a framework. You can plug in different topics or insights. They keep a structure that you know resonates with your audience.

Let's take a closer look at some proven templates you can use.

3. Utilize the Four Types of Engaging Posts

Let's cover the main four types of social media posts. Once you learn them, you can use them over and over again. Each type is designed to be engaging and get you those likes, comments, and shares. Remember, the goal is not to sell directly with these social media posts. The goal is to boost engagement and make yourself and your brand more visible.

Post Template 1. Educate Me (How-To Posts)

Educational content is a cornerstone of valuable social media content. These posts provide practical, actionable advice that your followers can apply as soon as possible.

Focus on posts that deliver how-to, practical advice, and step-by-step blueprints. By consistently offering this content, you become a trusted expert. This will encourage followers to return for more valuable insights.

Structure your how-to posts clearly:

- Start with a compelling headline: "5 Steps to Master [Skill]"

- Break down the process into clear, manageable steps

- Use bullet points or numbered lists for easy readability

- Include tips or common pitfalls to watch out for

- End with a call-to-action, encouraging followers to try the technique

Here's an example template:

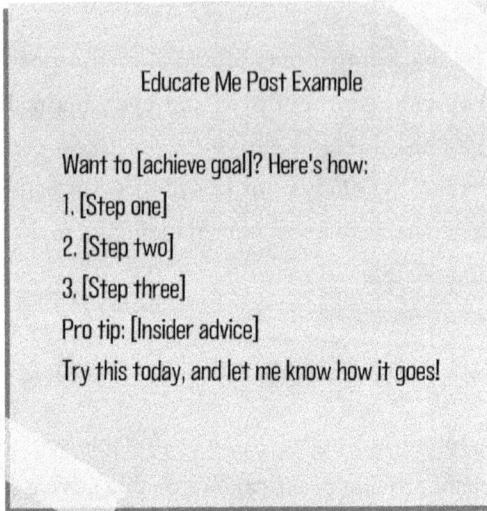

Educate Me Post Example

Want to [achieve goal]? Here's how:
1. [Step one]
2. [Step two]
3. [Step three]
Pro tip: [Insider advice]
Try this today, and let me know how it goes!

Once you have a template, you can reuse it repeatedly with new topics. Here's an example of one of my actual "Educate Me" posts:

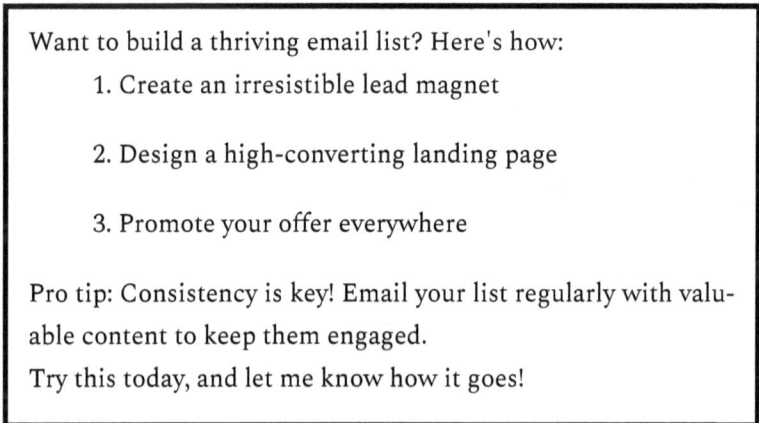

Want to build a thriving email list? Here's how:
    1. Create an irresistible lead magnet

    2. Design a high-converting landing page

    3. Promote your offer everywhere

Pro tip: Consistency is key! Email your list regularly with valuable content to keep them engaged.
Try this today, and let me know how it goes!

Post Template 2. Entertain Me (Stories with Lessons)

Stories captivate audiences and make your content more memorable. The key is to tell engaging stories that provide value through their lessons or morals.

Guidelines for compelling story posts:

- Start with a hook that grabs attention

- Keep the story concise and relevant

- Build tension or curiosity

- Clearly articulate the lesson or takeaway

- Relate the story to your audience's experiences or goals

Here's an example template:

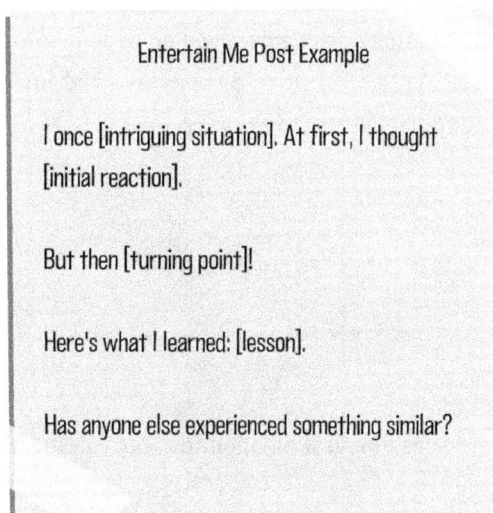

> **Entertain Me Post Example**
>
> I once [intriguing situation]. At first, I thought [initial reaction].
>
> But then [turning point]!
>
> Here's what I learned: [lesson].
>
> Has anyone else experienced something similar?

Now, here's an actual example of how I would use this template.

> I once sat down to write my first book. At first, I thought it would be a breeze - I mean, how hard could it be to just type out my ideas?
>
> But then I stared at the blank page for 3 hours straight, my cursor blinking mockingly at me!
>
> Here's what I learned: Writing a book is like trying to herd cats while juggling flaming torches... blindfolded.
>
> It's chaotic, unpredictable, and somehow both terrifying and exhilarating at the same time. But man, is it worth it when you finally type "The End"!
>
> Has anyone else experienced something similar in their writing journey? Share your stories below!

Post Template 3. Empower Me (Contrarian Views)

Sharing unique perspectives can set you apart and stimulate engaging discussions. The goal isn't to be controversial for its own sake but to offer thoughtful alternative viewpoints.

Tips for contrarian posts:

- Choose topics relevant to your niche

- Present your view respectfully and back it with logic or evidence

- Invite discussion and be open to other perspectives

- Focus on empowering your audience with new ways of thinking

Here's an example template:

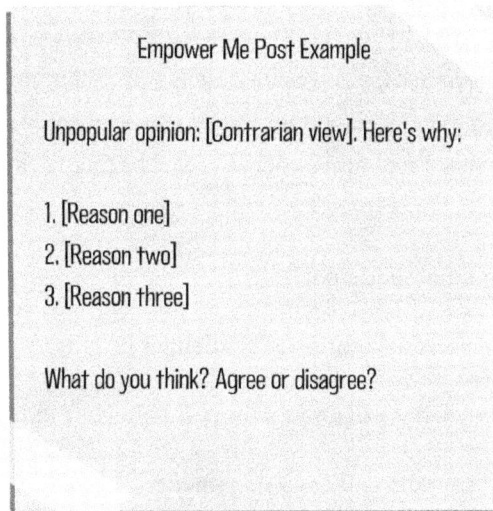

```
Empower Me Post Example

Unpopular opinion: [Contrarian view]. Here's why:

1. [Reason one]
2. [Reason two]
3. [Reason three]

What do you think? Agree or disagree?
```

Here's an example of how I would use this "Empower Me" post template:

> Unpopular opinion: Traditional book publishing is overrated. Here's why:
>
>   1. Creative control is limited. Your vision might get lost in the publisher's agenda.
>
>   2. The royalties are tiny. Most authors earn pennies per book sold.
>
>   3. The process is slow. It can take years from manuscript to bookshelf.
>
> What do you think? Agree or disagree?

Post Template 4. Empathize with Me (Relatable Content)

Empathetic posts connect by showing your human side. They acknowledge shared struggles. By opening up about your own challenges or experiences, you create a sense of community and trust with your audience. This vulnerability can lead to deeper engagement, as followers feel more comfortable sharing their own stories and perspectives in response.

Strategies for empathetic posts:

- Share personal stories of challenges or failures

- Acknowledge common pain points in your industry

- Offer support and encouragement

Here's an example template:

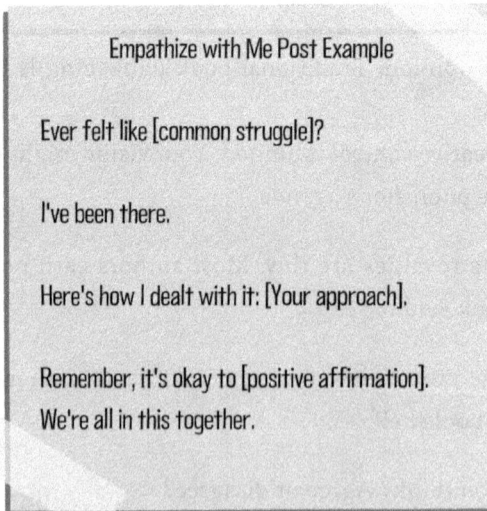

Empathize with Me Post Example

Ever felt like [common struggle]?

I've been there.

Here's how I dealt with it: [Your approach].

Remember, it's okay to [positive affirmation].
We're all in this together.

Here's an example of how I would use the "Empathize with Me" post template:

> Ever felt like your marketing efforts are falling on deaf ears? I've been there.
>
> Here's how I dealt with it: I started sharing more personal stories - like Shasta (our Husky) photobombing my coaching calls!
>
> Remember, it's okay to feel unseen sometimes. Your message matters, even when it seems no one's listening.
>
> We're all in this together. Keep showing up, keep being you.
>
> How do you handle feeling invisible? Let's chat!

4. Craft Compelling Headlines and Hooks

Your opening lines are crucial in the fast-paced world of social media. Craft headlines and hooks that stop the scroll and compel followers to read more.

Techniques for attention-grabbing openings:

- Ask a thought-provoking question

- Start with a surprising statistic or fact

- Make a bold statement

- Use "How to" or numbered list formats

- Create curiosity with an incomplete idea

5. Optimize for Each Platform

Your message may stay the same. But, you must optimize your posts for each platform's features and audience.

Platform-specific tips:

- Twitter: Use threads for longer content, incorporate relevant hashtags

- LinkedIn: Start with a compelling first line, use paragraph breaks for readability

- Instagram: Pair your caption with an eye-catching image or carousel post

- Facebook: Longer posts can work well, but still prioritize readability with paragraphs and emojis

6. Engage with Your Audience

Posting consistently is just the first step. Engage your audience. Respond to comments, ask questions, and foster discussions.

Some engagement strategies include:

- Respond to comments promptly and thoughtfully

- Ask open-ended questions in your posts to encourage responses

- Use polls or other interactive features when available

- Share and comment on your followers' content when relevant

7. Analyze and Adjust

Review your post performance regularly to understand what resonates with your audience. Use platform analytics to track engagement rate, reach, and follower growth metrics.

Here's a few key metrics to monitor:

- Engagement rate (likes, comments, shares)

- Reach and impressions

- Follower growth

- Click-through rates (if applicable)

These insights can help you refine your strategy, doubling down on what works and adjusting what doesn't.

Today's Exercise: Crafting Your First Set of Template Posts

In this exercise, you'll create four social media posts, one for each of the template types we've discussed. This will help you practice using these templates and give you a head start on your daily posting strategy.

1. Choose your primary social media platform. This is where you'll be posting your content.

2. For each of the four post types (Educate, Entertain, Empower, and Empathize), write one post. Use the templates provided in the chapter as a guide, but feel free to adapt them to your style and niche.

3. Educate Me (How-To Post):

Write a post that teaches your audience how to do something related to your field of expertise. Remember to start with a compelling headline, break down the process into clear steps, and end with a call-to-action.

4. Entertain Me (Story with a Lesson):

Craft a post that tells a brief, engaging story with a valuable lesson for your audience. Begin with a hook, keep the story concise, and clearly articulate the takeaway.

5. Empower Me (Contrarian View):

Develop a post that presents a unique perspective on a topic in your niche. Present your view respectfully, back it with logic or evidence, and invite discussion.

6. Empathize with Me (Relatable Content):

Create a post that shows your human side and acknowledges a common struggle in your industry. Share a personal challenge or experience, and offer support or encouragement.

7. After writing your posts, review them to ensure they're optimized for your chosen platform. Pay special attention to your headlines and opening lines.

8. If you feel comfortable, share one or more of these posts on your chosen platform. Observe how your audience responds and engage with any comments you receive.

9. Reflect on the process. Which type of post felt most natural to write? Which do you think will resonate most with your audience?

Remember, the goal is to practice using these templates and start building your daily posting habit. Don't aim for perfection – focus on creating valuable content that serves your audience.

Key Takeaways:

- Consistency is key: Commit to posting valuable content daily to build trust and stay top-of-mind with your audience.

- Variety engages: Use different post types to keep your content fresh and exciting. Educate, entertain, empower, and empathize.

- Value first: Focus on providing genuine value to your audience rather than direct promotion. The relationships and trust you build will lead to business opportunities.

8

The Video Shorts Traffic Playbook

I n a small Italian town, an unlikely star was born amidst the chaos of a global pandemic. Khaby Lame, a factory worker turned TikTok sensation, found himself jobless and restless. He started creating with nothing but time on his hands and a smartphone in his pocket.

Khaby's videos weren't flashy, and they didn't need to be. His wordless, deadpan reactions to overly complicated life hacks struck a chord globally. No language barrier could stop the universal appeal of his exasperated looks and simple solutions.

From zero to 150 million followers. Let that sink in. That's more than twice the population of Italy, all tuning in to watch short, silent videos of a guy making fun of ridiculous life hacks.[6]

Khaby's meteoric rise isn't just a feel-good story. It's a masterclass in modern audience building. He proved that, with creativity and consistency, anyone can build a huge following through short videos. A keen understanding of what people want is key.

This is the new frontier of digital communication. Platforms like TikTok, Instagram Reels, and YouTube Shorts aren't just trends. They're changing how we connect, entertain, and influence.

In this chapter, we will unpack the power of video shorts. We'll explore why they dominate social media. We'll also look at how different platforms embrace them. Most importantly, we'll discuss how to use their potential to grow your audience.

Short and Sweet: Why Your Long-Form Strategy Is Costing You Views

Let's talk about what most people are doing wrong. Many content creators are stuck in old habits, churning long-form content without adapting to new trends. They're like someone trying to sell encyclopedias in a world of Google searches. These creators often post infrequently. Their audience is left wondering when they'll hear from them next. And here's another common mistake: they create one piece of content and blast it across all platforms without tweaks. It's like wearing a tuxedo to a beach party - it doesn't fit.

Why doesn't this approach work? For starters, our attention spans are shrinking faster than a wool sweater in a hot dryer. We're bombarded with information 24/7, and long-form content often gets scrolled past. Plus, social media algorithms have a clear preference: they love short, engaging content that keeps users on the platform. By sticking to old methods, creators miss out on countless opportunities for their content to go viral and reach new audiences.

So, what should you do differently? It's time for a mental shift. Embrace the world of short-form video across multiple platforms. Think of it as crafting bite-sized, irresistible snacks for your audience instead of serving a seven-course meal. Create a consistent posting strategy - your audience should know when to expect your content, like their favorite TV show. And here's the kicker: optimize your content for each platform's unique features and audience. It's not one-size-fits-all anymore. You need to speak the language of each platform to truly connect with your audience.

Remember, in short-form video, you're not just competing with other creators in your niche. You're up against every cute cat video, every viral dance trend, and every "oddly satisfying" clip. You need to play the game smarter, not harder, to stand out.

Step 1: Understand the Short-Form Video Landscape

The digital world has a new darling: videos that are 60 seconds or less. These bite-sized snippets have taken over our feeds, capturing attention in a world where time is our most precious commodity. To thrive in this landscape, you need to know the lay of the land.

TikTok, Instagram Stories, Facebook Stories, YouTube Shorts, and LinkedIn each have their own take on short-form content. They're like different neighborhoods in the city of social media, each with its own culture and language. Get to know them. Spend time on each platform, observing what works and what falls flat.

Think of short-form videos as modern-day newspaper headlines. They need to grab attention quickly and convey a message efficiently. In a sea of content, your video needs to be the one that makes thumbs stop scrolling.

Mastering this format isn't just a nice-to-have anymore. It's essential for building a solid online presence in today's digital landscape. Ignore it; you risk becoming as relevant as a flip phone in the smartphone world.

Step 2: Develop a Content Strategy

Now that you understand the landscape, it's time to map out your journey. Who are you trying to reach? What makes them tick? Your target audience isn't just a demographic; they're people with preferences. Get to know them like you'd get to know a friend.

Next, create a content calendar. Consistency is key in the world of short-form video. As Gary Vaynerchuk famously said, "Content is king, but consistency is queen." Your audience should know when to expect your content, like when their favorite TV show drops new episodes.

Plan a mix of content that entertains, educates, and promotes. Think of it as a balanced diet for your audience's content consumption. Too much of one type, and they'll lose interest. Strike the right balance, and they'll keep coming back for more.

Remember, a well-planned content strategy isn't just about what you post - it's about building a relationship with your audience. It's the difference between shouting into the void and having a conversation.

Step 3: Create Short Videos from Long Videos

Do you have long-form content? Don't let it gather dust. Tools like Opus.pro are your new best friend. They can extract the most viral-worthy 60 seconds from your longer videos, giving you a goldmine of short-form content.

But don't stop there. Adapt these snippets for different platforms. What works on TikTok might need a tweak for LinkedIn. It's like translating a joke - the punchline needs to land in any language.

Cross-promote your content across all your social media channels. It's like being your own hype man. The more places your content lives, the more chances it has to be seen and shared.

Step 4: Leverage Platform-Specific Features

Each platform has its own secret sauce. Hashtags, sounds, effects - these aren't just bells and whistles. They're powerful tools to boost your visibility.

Participate in trending challenges and topics. It's like joining a conversation at a party - it helps you connect with others and shows you're in the know.

Use platform-specific tools. TikTok's Duet feature, for example, is a goldmine for engagement. It's like having a dialogue with your audience but in video form.

Remember the birth of the hashtag on Twitter in 2007? It revolutionized how we discover content on social media. Today's platform-specific features are doing the same thing. Master them, and you'll significantly boost your content's visibility and engagement.

In short, leveraging these features is about more than just being trendy. It's about speaking the native language of each platform. Do it well, and you'll not just be part of the conversation - you'll be leading it.

Today's Exercise: Create Your First 60-second Video

Ready to put your new knowledge into action? Let's create a 60-second video to make waves across three social media platforms.

Start by crafting your message. Who are you? What's your brand all about? Distill your essence into a punchy, engaging narrative that fits into 60 seconds. Remember, you're not writing a novel here - you're creating a trailer for your personal brand.

Now, grab your smartphone. Don't worry about fancy equipment—authenticity trumps production value in short-form video. Find a well-lit spot with a clean background. Take a deep breath, and hit record.

Once you've got your raw video, it's time to optimize for different platforms. Let's tackle three: TikTok, Instagram Reels, and LinkedIn.

For TikTok, add some trending music in the background. Use text overlays to emphasize key points—remember, many users watch with the sound off. End with a strong call to action, encouraging viewers to follow you for more content.

On Instagram Reels, focus on visual appeal. Use Instagram's built-in filters to give your video a polished look. Add relevant hashtags in your caption to boost discoverability.

For LinkedIn, keep it professional but personable. Use captions to provide context and highlight your expertise. Consider adding subtitles. They're vital for accessibility and for viewers scrolling silently during their workday.

Post your videos and pay attention to the engagement on each platform. Which version resonates most with your audience? Use these insights to refine your approach for future content.

Remember, this isn't about perfection - it's about getting started. Your first attempt might feel awkward, but that's okay. The beauty of short-form video is that you can always create another one tomorrow. So go ahead, put yourself out there. Your audience is waiting to meet you.

Key Takeaways:

- Embrace the power of short-form video content to grow your audience and increase online visibility rapidly.

- Consistency, quality, and platform-specific optimization are crucial to a successful video shorts strategy.

- Engage your audience, analyze performance, and adapt to stay relevant in the fast-changing digital world.

9

The Private Facebook Group Traffic Playbook

L andon Stewart and Chris Stapleton weren't always the success stories they are today. Hailing from a small farm town in
Illinois and working as bartenders in Connecticut, these two had
their fair share of failed businesses. However, their fortunes changed
when they met at a marketing event hosted by Mark Hoverson in
2015.

Under Mark's wing, Landon and Chris learned the ropes of manag-
ing a Facebook group with 2,000 clients. They honed their skills in
engaging and rallying a community - little did they know how crucial
this experience would be.

Fast-forward to 2018. After Mark's passing, Landon and Chris found
themselves in a tight spot financially. But their entrepreneurial spirit
wouldn't let them give up. In January 2019, they launched their
first Facebook group, Social Media Entrepreneurs. Within a year, it
exploded to 18,000 members and generated significant revenue.

Riding a wave of success, they founded Clients & Community in January 2020. It focused on teaching others to grow profitable Facebook
groups. Their methods gained quick fame. They got speaking gigs
with industry giants like Tony Robbins and Russell Brunson. By July
2022, Clients & Community had raked in over $10 million in revenue,
with their clients collectively earning more than $100 million.[7]

Pretty impressive, right? But here's the kicker: you don't need to be a marketing guru or have a huge following to replicate this success. The secret is to leverage private Facebook groups.

This chapter will explore private Facebook groups. They can help you build a dedicated audience, grow your email list, and generate revenue. Why is this important? Because your audience is already on Facebook! You're tapping into an existing user base. You're creating a community around your niche or business. You're doing this by providing a space for them to engage with you and like-minded people.

Ready to unlock the potential of private Facebook groups? Let's get started!

What Most People Get Wrong When Starting a Facebook Group

Many well-intentioned creators stumble when launching their Facebook groups. They're excited about building a community but often miss the mark on key elements that make a group thrive.

Mistake 1. The Open Door Policy

One common misstep is creating a public group with no entry barriers. It seems logical – more members mean more engagement, right? Not quite. Without any filtering, you might end up with a mismatched crowd that doesn't align with your group's purpose. It's like throwing a party and forgetting to send invitations – you never know who might show up.

Mistake 2. The Silent Treatment

Another frequent mistake is neglecting to foster engagement. Some creators build a group and expect members to start chatting automatically. But without consistent, valuable content and discussion prompts, a group can quickly turn into a ghost town. Members need a reason to participate, share, and return.

Mistake 3. The Self-Promotion Trap

Perhaps the most off-putting error is turning the group into a non-stop promotional channel. It's tempting to use your group to promote your products. But, overwhelming members with sales pitches will drive them away. People join groups to connect, learn, and share—not to be constantly sold to.

By avoiding these common pitfalls, you're already ahead of the game. Remember, a successful Facebook group is about creating value for your members, not just for yourself. It's about building a community, not an audience. Keep this in mind, and you'll be well on your way to creating a thriving, engaged Facebook group that members love to be part of.

Building a Facebook Group People Love

Want to create a Facebook group that thrives? Think of it as an exclusive VIP club. Make your group's purpose clear and enticing. Members should feel special, part of something unique.

Be the host who keeps the party going. Serve up engaging content consistently. Mix it up with insights, questions, and debates. Keep your members excited to return.

Focus on relationships first and business second. Build trust and genuine connections. Give freely of your knowledge and time. Business opportunities will naturally follow when you've nurtured a community that values you.

Remember, creating a successful Facebook group is a long game. It's about building a community that enriches lives. Do this well, and you'll cultivate a tribe of loyal fans and potential customers.

Step 1: Define Your Group's Purpose and Target Audience

What's your superpower? What can you offer that no one else can? Maybe you're a fitness guru for busy moms or a tech whiz for seniors. Find your sweet spot and own it.

Get inside your audience's head. What keeps them up at night? What do they dream about? If you were a mind reader, what would you see? This insight is gold.

Now, craft your group's elevator pitch. Make it snappy, clear, and irresistible. If your ideal member stumbled upon your group, would they hit "Join" without hesitation?

Think of your Facebook group as a themed party. The more specific and interesting the theme, the more excited and engaged your guests will be. A "pizza party" is okay, but a "build-your-own-gourmet-pizza night with a professional chef"? Now that's a party people will talk about!

Step 2: Set Up Your Private Group with Strategic Entry Questions

Your entry questions are your VIP bouncer. Make sure only the right people get in. Ask about their biggest challenges, goals, and experience levels. Get creative!

Sneaky? Nah. Smart? Absolutely. Include a question to capture email addresses. This is your ticket to building a relationship beyond Facebook's walls.

What do they hope to get from the group? This info is like a compass guiding your content strategy.

Remember what Jimmy Johnson said: "The difference between ordinary and extraordinary is that little extra." Your entry questions are that extra. They ensure quality members and provide valuable data for audience building.

A well-defined purpose attracts the right audience and sets the foundation for a thriving community. It's like planting seeds in fertile soil—with the proper care, they'll grow into something beautiful.

Step 3: Grow Your Facebook Group Fast

You've set the stage. Now it's time to fill the seats. Let's explore seven powerful strategies to skyrocket your group's growth.

1. Use the "Common Groups" Feature

Ever wonder where to find your ideal members? They're already in groups! Use the "Common Groups" feature to target people already interested in your topic.

Click that blue "Invite" button on your group. Select "Groups in common." Search for groups in your niche. Boom! You'll see friends who are members of these related groups. Invite away!

2. Leverage Your Facebook Fan Page

Do you have a Facebook fan page? It's time to make it work for you. Link your group to your page. Use the "Invite" feature to invite followers to your group. Here's a pro tip: enable automatic invites for top fans and recently active followers.

3. Create a Pinned Post on Your Fan Page

Create a compelling post inviting people to join your group. Include the link. Now, pin it to the top of your fan page. This pinned post is visible to every visitor to your page and works for you 24/7.

4. Optimize Your Personal Facebook Profile

Your personal profile is often the first impression people have of you online. Edit your intro to include a call-to-action and link to your group. Create and pin a post about your group on your personal profile.

5. Engage in Other Facebook Groups

Choose five groups with your target audience. Regularly answer questions and provide value. Optimize your "group profile" for each group you're active in. Change your cover photo to promote your group.

6. Use Email Marketing

Your email list is full of potential group members. Include a link to your Facebook group in your welcome email sequence. Regularly promote valuable group content to your email list.

7. Cross-Promote with Facebook Posts

Create valuable, engaging posts in your Facebook group. Then, share these posts via email, encouraging list subscribers to join the group for more content.

Remember, growing your group isn't about quick fixes. It's about consistent, strategic effort. Keep at it, and watch your community flourish!

Today's Exercise: Map Out the Vision for Your Facebook Group

Ready to turn your Facebook group idea into reality? Let's roll up our sleeves and get to work. This exercise will help you lay the foundation for a thriving online community.

Start by carving out 15 minutes of uninterrupted time. Grab a pen and paper or open your favorite note-taking app. We're going to define your group's DNA.

Step 1. Define Your Group's Purpose

First, let's tackle your group's purpose. Write down 3-5 sentences describing why your group exists. Ask yourself: What problem does your group solve? What value does it provide? Keep refining it until it feels precise and compelling. This is your group's north star.

Step 2. Create Your Ideal Member Persona

Next, let's paint a picture of your ideal member. Create a brief persona. Who are they? What are their interests? What challenges do they face? What are their goals? Be as specific as possible. Remember, you can't please everyone!

Step 3. Craft Your Entry Questions

Now, let's consider how you'll welcome new members. Brainstorm 5-7 potential entry questions. These should align with your group's purpose and target audience. Pick your top 3. Make sure one of these aims to capture email addresses—this will be invaluable for growing your community beyond Facebook.

Step 4. Bring Your Vision to Life

Finally, it's time to bring your vision to life. Head over to Facebook and set up your group. Use the purpose, target audience, and entry questions you've just crafted.

Step 5. Review and Refine

Take a step back and review your plan. Does it excite you? Great! That energy will shine through in your group. If not, keep refining until it does. Your future group members are waiting for you to create this amazing space for them.

Remember, a well-defined group attracts the right people and sets the stage for meaningful interactions. You're not just creating a Facebook group but building a community. Now, go make it happen!

Key Takeaways:

- A private Facebook group with a clear purpose attracts quality members who are likelier to engage and convert.

- To grow your audience, you must engage them. You need to post valuable content and manage your community actively.

- Using Facebook group features and cross-promotion can greatly boost group growth and engagement.

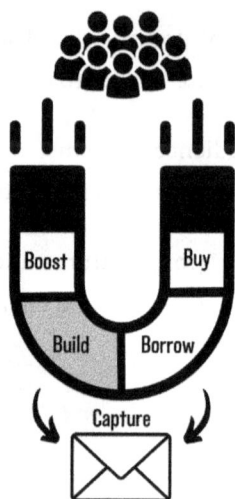

The Build Method
(Search Traffic)

10

The Blogging Traffic Playbook

M y fingers were shaking the day I hit publish on my first blog post. It was February 2009, and I'd just launched a career coaching blog for accounting professionals. After five years as an executive recruiter, I learned a ton about job transitions and career advancement. Now, I wanted to share that knowledge and make some money doing it.

Why blogging? My research said it was the best way to reach people. So, I started writing about the questions I got daily—resumes, interviews, salary negotiations, you name it.

What happened next blew my mind. Within 90 days, emails started pouring in—not just from around the country but from across the globe. That's when I knew I was onto something big. It was time to double down on blogging and figure out how to turn this into a real business.

But here's the thing—building an audience through blogging isn't as simple as writing whatever pops into your head and hoping people show up. There's a strategy to it, a method that can turn your blog from a ghost town into a bustling hub of engaged readers.

In this chapter, we will explore how to build your audience through blogging. We'll look at common mistakes and better ways to write. Then, we'll give you a step-by-step guide to creating content that attracts and keeps readers. Ready to turn your blog into an audience-building machine? Let's get started.

The Common Pitfall: What Most Bloggers Do Wrong

Ever feel like you're shouting into the void with your blog? You're not alone. Most bloggers fall into a common trap that keeps their audience small and engagement low.

Here's what they do wrong:

They treat their blog like a diary. Every post is a personal musing or a deep thought they just had to share. It's all "me, me, me" and not enough "you, you, you."

Or they try to be thought leaders right out of the gate. They write grand manifestos and expect the world to sit up and take notice.

Then they hit publish, and... crickets. They sit back and wait for readers to appear magically. After all, if you build it, they will come. Right?

Wrong.

This approach fails spectacularly for those starting in obscurity. Why? Because no one is looking for your random thoughts. They're looking for solutions to their problems.

A Better Approach: Become a Topic Leader

So what's the secret sauce? Becoming a topic leader.

Shift your focus. Instead of writing about what's on your mind, write about what's on your audience's mind. What questions are they asking? What problems are they facing?

Build topical authority in your niche. Don't try to be everything to everyone. Pick your lane and own it. Dive deep into your chosen topics and become the go-to expert.

Leverage SEO. People use search engines to find answers. If you want to be found, you need to speak their language and use the keywords and phrases they're searching for.

Remember: People don't go to Google typing "Jane Doe's latest thought piece." They type "How do I fix my leaky faucet?" or "Best ways to lose belly fat."

You're not just throwing content into the void by focusing on these searched topics. You're creating a beacon that draws your audience to you.

Becoming a topic leader isn't about being the loudest voice. It's about being the most helpful voice. When you consistently provide value, your audience will grow. And with that growth comes the opportunity to share your unique insights and perspectives.

So stop waiting for readers to find you. Start creating content they're actively searching for. That's how you build an audience with blogging.

The P.O.S.T. Method: A Framework for Quality Blog Posts

Ready to create blog posts that attract and engage readers? Let's dive into the P.O.S.T. method. It's your secret weapon for crafting content that stands out in the crowded blogosphere.

Purpose: Defining Your Post's Core

Start with your primary keyword. What's the core topic you're addressing? Use this to craft a compelling title.

Your title is your first impression. Make it count. Aim for 47-53 characters. Why? That's the sweet spot for search engine results pages.

Think of your title like a newspaper headline. It needs to grab attention and make people want to read more. Your blog post title is like a shop window - it must entice people to enter.

Outline: Structuring Your Content

Now that you have your headline, use it as a guide to outline your main points. What key ideas will support your purpose?

Remember, a well-structured outline is the skeleton of a great blog post. It gives your content shape and direction.

Break your ideas into clear sections. This makes your post easier to write and easier to read.

Strengthen: Enhancing SEO and User Experience

It's time to beef up your post. Use tools like RankIQ or NeuronWriter to optimize your keywords. These tools can show you what words and phrases to include for better search engine rankings.

Don't forget visuals. Add relevant images to break up text and illustrate your points.

Link it up. Include external links to authoritative sources and internal links to your other relevant posts.

Create strong metadata. This is what appears in search results. A compelling meta description can be the difference between a click and a pass.

Think of SEO as the roadmap that guides readers to your content on the vast internet. Without it, even the best content can get lost.

Tidy Up: Polishing Your Post

You're in the home stretch. Now it's time to make your post shine.

Edit ruthlessly. Cut unnecessary words. Clarify confusing points. Break up long paragraphs for better readability.

Add calls to action. What do you want readers to do next? Do you want them to subscribe to your newsletter? Make it clear and compelling.

Remember, editing is not just about fixing errors; it's about making your content shine. It's your last chance to make your post as impactful as possible.

The P.O.S.T. method isn't just about creating content. It's about creating content with purpose, structure, and polish. It's your framework for blog posts that attract readers and keep them coming back for more.

Advanced Blogging Practices for Accelerated Results

Ready to kick your blogging into high gear? Let's explore some advanced techniques that can supercharge your results.

Pillar Posts: Cornerstones of Your Blog

Think of pillar posts as the foundation of your blog. These comprehensive, in-depth articles cover your niche's major topics. Aim to create 12-15 of these powerhouse posts.

For a blogging-focused blog, pillar posts might include:

• How to Start a Blog

• Monetizing Your Blog

• Driving Traffic to Your Blog

• Creating Compelling Content

These posts are typically longer and more detailed than your average post. They're the content you want to be known for.

Support Posts: Building a Content Ecosystem

Now, let's flesh out your content ecosystem with support posts. These are subtopics that link back to your pillar posts.

For the "How to Start a Blog" pillar, support posts could include:

• Choosing the Right Blogging Platform

• 50 Blog Post Ideas for Beginners

• How Often Should You Post on Your Blog?

Each support post links back to its pillar, which in turn links out to all its support posts. This creates a web of interlinked content that search engines love.

Why does this work? It establishes your topical authority. You're showing search engines (and readers) that you have comprehensive coverage of your niche.

Content Strategy Management

Here's where the rubber meets the road. To keep all this organized, create a blog content strategy spreadsheet.

Track:

• Post titles

• Post types (pillar or support)

• Publication dates

• Interlinking status

This might seem overkill, but trust me, it's a game-changer. A well-organized content strategy is like a map for your blogging journey - it keeps you on track and heading in the right direction.

With pillar posts, support posts, and a solid content strategy, you're not just blogging anymore. You're building a content empire. It should attract readers, show your expertise, and ensure long-term success.

Remember, these are advanced techniques. Don't feel pressured to implement them all at once. Start with one pillar post and a few support posts. As you get comfortable, expand your strategy. Before you know it, you'll have a robust, interconnected blog that draws readers in and keeps them returning for more.

Today's Exercise: One-Day Blog Post Challenge

Ready to put your new knowledge into action? Let's create a blog post from scratch in just one day. This exercise will help you apply the P.O.S.T. method and get a feel for the entire process.

Here's your challenge:

Start by choosing a topic relevant to your niche. Think about questions your audience frequently asks or problems they often face. If you're stuck, browse forums or social media groups related to your niche to see what people are discussing.

Next, apply the P.O.S.T. method to create your blog post. Begin with purpose: define your main keyword and craft a compelling title. Then, create an outline of your main points. Strengthen your post by using a keyword research tool like RankIQ or NeuronWriter to optimize your content. Finally, tidy up by editing your post for clarity and readability.

When your post is ready, hit publish. Don't let perfectionism hold you back - remember, done is better than perfect. Once it's live, share it on one social media platform where your target audience hangs out.

The goal isn't to create a masterpiece but to practice the process. Pay attention to what feels challenging and what comes naturally. This will help you identify areas for improvement and build your blogging muscles.

After you've completed the challenge, take a few minutes to reflect. What did you learn? What would you do differently next time? Use these insights to refine your process for future posts.

Remember, blogging is a skill that improves with practice. The more you write, the better you'll become at crafting posts that resonate with your audience and attract new readers. So, are you ready to take on this one-day blog post challenge?

Key Takeaways:

- Successful blogging addresses your audience's needs and questions, not just sharing personal thoughts.

- The P.O.S.T. method (Purpose, Outline, Strengthen, Tidy Up) provides a structured approach to creating SEO-friendly, engaging blog posts.

- Advanced practices like pillar and support posts can boost your blog's visibility. They can also establish your authority on the topic.

11

The Medium Traffic Playbook

B enjamin Hardy started blogging seriously in May 2015. His blog had no audience, just his wife. As discussed in the last chapter, you can't just publish your thoughts on a blog and get traction. To be successful with a blog, you must focus on SEO. What Benjamin needed was a platform designed for thought leaders. So, he started publishing on Medium. In six months, he went from zero to 20,000 subscribers. How? By using the platform's unique ecosystem of curious minds. They crave thought-provoking content.

Medium is a platform where content is king. It's not about connections or existing platforms. High-quality content rises to the top. Hardy's articles on Medium drew massive traffic. One went viral, drawing 200,000 clicks per day. His subscriber count shot up. He added a call-to-action to his posts, inviting readers to subscribe. His followers grew exponentially.

Hardy's success wasn't just luck. He experimented with his writing, framing goals as quests and creating content that couldn't be ignored. He focused on quantity and quality, using listicles, research, and powerful quotes. He knew that great content on Medium could lead to more significant opportunities. Business Insider, Huffington Post, and The Observer republished his work. This strategy built his audience and credibility.[8]

This chapter will show you how to replicate Hardy's success on Medium. Medium is about sharing new ideas, trends, and insights, unlike a traditional blog relying on SEO. Medium already has an audience craving thought leadership. You'll learn how to use Medium to build an audience and an email list and even earn money, just like Hardy did.

Ready to turn your ideas into a thriving audience? Let's dive in and unlock the secrets of Medium success.

The Medium Mistake

You've just joined Medium and are excited to share your expertise. You want to make your mark. So, you approach it like your Word-Press blog. You churn out SEO-optimized articles that answer the most common questions in your field. But as you hit publish, you're met with silence. No views, no claps, no comments. What gives?

The hard truth is that Medium isn't your average blog platform. Treating it as such is a surefire way to fade into obscurity. Most newcomers fall into a traditional trap, making several critical mistakes. They copy-paste their existing blog content, expecting instant success. Some obsess over SEO. They stuff their articles with keywords. They forget there's a human on the other side of the screen. Perhaps worst of all, many ignore Medium's unique audience. They write what they want, not what Medium readers crave.

These approaches flop because they misunderstand Medium's secret sauce: its audience. Medium readers aren't your typical Google searchers. They're curious explorers hungry for fresh perspectives, cutting-edge ideas, and personal insights. They want to read about your experiments, failures, and breakthroughs. SEO-driven content feels stale here. It doesn't spark conversations or inspire shares—the lifeblood of Medium's success.

Medium's algorithms favor engaging, thought-provoking content. Dry, keyword-stuffed articles sink faster than a stone in a pond. To win on Medium, you need to think like a thought leader. Be a trendspotter, sharing emerging ideas in your field before they hit the mainstream. Experiment publicly, documenting your journey with honesty and vulnerability. Engage rather than lecture, starting conversations, asking questions, and inviting debate.

On Medium, quality reigns supreme. Craft each sentence carefully, infusing your unique voice and experiences into every piece. Medium readers crave substance, not fluff. Give them meaty ideas to chew on, and they will return for seconds, thirds, and more. Embrace Medium's unique ecosystem. It can turn you from a struggling newbie into a respected expert.

The Thought Leader Approach

To truly thrive on Medium, you need to adopt the mindset of a thought leader. This means being more than a source of information. You must be a beacon of new ideas and perspectives in your field. Start by honing your ability to spot emerging trends before they hit the mainstream. Share these insights with your readers, giving them a sneak peek into the future of your industry.

Don't be afraid to experiment publicly. Medium readers love to follow along on a journey of discovery. Document your trials, your failures, and your breakthroughs. Being vulnerable and open will endear you to your audience. It will make your content more relatable and engaging.

Remember, engagement is key on Medium. Instead of lecturing your readers, strive to start conversations. Ask thought-provoking questions and invite debate. Your goal should be to create a community around your ideas, not just a passive readership. Quality should be at the forefront of everything you write.

Your Medium Success Roadmap

Think of Medium as YouTube for writers. Successful vloggers build loyal audiences with engaging videos. You'll attract followers with captivating articles. Medium isn't just another blogging platform. It's a vibrant ideas marketplace. Readers seek fresh perspectives there. Approach it with this unique ecosystem in mind, and you'll be miles ahead of the competition.

Step 1. Craft Content That Captivates

As a Medium superstar, Benjamin Hardy often says, "Content really is king." On Medium, this rings truer than ever. The most successful writers on the platform don't simply rehash common knowledge. Instead, they share new ideas, document bold experiments, and spot trends before they hit the mainstream. Your goal should be to create compelling content so readers can't help but click that "Follow" button.

Step 2. Ride the Publication Wave

Imagine getting your article in front of 100,000+ engaged readers overnight - that's the power of Medium publications. Hardy skyrocketed his visibility by publishing in top outlets like The Mission. He did this by crafting articles that matched each publication's audience and guidelines. Start small, then work your way up to the heavy hitters. Each published piece is a stepping stone to a broader audience.

Step 3. Polish Your Presence

Your Medium profile is your digital storefront, so make it shine. Use attention-grabbing headlines and high-quality images, and format your articles for easy reading. A polished, professional look tells readers you're serious about your craft. Remember, a study from MIT found that articles with images get 94% more views than those without. Apply this logic to your entire Medium presence.

Step 4. Join the Conversation

Medium thrives on community. Engage like the literary salons of old Paris—where great minds gathered to spark new ideas. Leave thoughtful comments on articles in your niche, follow writers who inspire you, and respond to comments on your own work. Every interaction is a chance to expand your network and attract new readers.

Step 5. Consistency is Key

"Quantity is the most likely path to quality," Hardy reminds us. It's simple math - the more you write, the higher your chances of creating a breakout hit. Set a publishing schedule and stick to it. Whether once a week or three times a month, your consistency will pay off in engaged readers eagerly awaiting your next piece.

Step 6. Grow Beyond Medium

Medium is powerful, but don't put all your eggs in one basket. Use it as a launchpad for a broader online presence. Hardy grew his email list to 20,000 subscribers in just six months using Medium. He achieved this by including compelling calls to action in his articles, offering readers even more value off-platform. Remember, your ultimate goal is to build lasting connections with your audience – wherever they prefer to engage with you.

Today's Exercise: Analyze Popular Medium Articles

Step 1: Select Three Popular Articles

Begin by selecting three popular Medium articles in your niche. Choose pieces that have garnered significant engagement through claps, comments, and shares. These articles will serve as your case studies.

Step 2: Identify Key Elements

Examine each article's title closely. Note how it captures attention and entices readers to click. Consider whether it poses a question, makes a bold statement, or offers a compelling list.

Next, analyze the structure of each piece. Observe how the author organizes their thoughts and maintains a coherent flow. Watch their opening strategies. Do they start with a personal anecdote, present research, or dive straight into the main points?

Evaluate the tone of each article. Determine if the writing style is conversational, authoritative, or perhaps infused with humor. Reflect on how this tone contributes to reader engagement. Don't forget to assess the call to action at the end of each article. Note how the author encourages interaction. They invite comments, request shares, and promote subscriptions.

Step 3: Outline Your First Medium Article

Now, use these insights to outline your own Medium article. Based on your observations, craft an attention-grabbing title. Write an engaging introduction that hooks readers from the start. Organize your main points with clear headings and subheadings. Conclude with a strong ending and a call to action that fosters reader engagement.

This exercise will deepen your understanding of effective Medium writing strategies. By analyzing successful articles, you'll find techniques that resonate with the platform's audience. Then, use those techniques in your content.

Key Takeaways:

- Medium is a unique platform. It requires a thought leadership approach, not traditional blogging tactics.

- To succeed on Medium, share new ideas and experiments. They should resonate with its reading-focused audience.

- Using Medium's ecosystem is vital to building a large audience and email list. This includes its publications and community engagement.

12

The Podcast Traffic Playbook

I t's 1895, and a young Italian inventor named Guglielmo Marconi is tinkering in his attic. He's obsessed with an almost magical idea - sending messages through the air without wires. Most people think he's crazy. After all, how could invisible waves possibly carry information across vast distances?

But Marconi isn't deterred. He keeps experimenting, refining his apparatus, pushing the boundaries of what's possible. And then, one day, it happens. He successfully transmits a radio signal over a distance of two miles. It's a small step but the beginning of a revolution.

Fast-forward a few years. Marconi's invention has grown by leaps and bounds. In 1901, he achieved what many thought impossible—transmitting a radio signal across the Atlantic Ocean. Suddenly, the world seems a whole lot smaller. News, entertainment, and information can travel at the speed of light.

Marconi's radio laid the foundation for a new era of communication. From those first crackling transmissions, we've evolved to crystal-clear digital broadcasts. And now? We're in the age of podcasting - where anyone with a microphone and an internet connection can reach listeners around the globe.[9]

It's a far cry from Marconi's attic experiments. But, the core principle is the same: using technology to share ideas and connect with an audience. Just as Marconi's radio revolutionized communication in his time, podcasting is transforming how we build audiences and share knowledge today.

The power of podcasting isn't just in its reach. It's in its intimacy. When someone listens to your podcast, it's like you're speaking directly to them. You're in their car, their living room, their workout routine. You're building a connection that goes beyond words on a page or images on a screen.

That's why podcasting has become such a potent tool for building an audience. It's not just about broadcasting information - it's about creating a relationship with your listeners. It's about being a trusted voice in your field. Do this by sharing business insights, telling great stories, or exploring niche topics.

In this chapter, we'll explore how you can harness the power of podcasting to build your own audience. We'll cover the steps to set up and launch a podcast. We'll also explore strategies to create a show that resonates with listeners and keeps them coming back.

So, are you ready to follow in Marconi's footsteps and start your own broadcasting revolution? Let's dive in and discover how you can use podcasting to build your audience and amplify your voice.

Avoid These Common Podcasting Mistakes

Many aspiring hosts fall into the same traps when it comes to podcasting. They overcomplicate the process, turning what should be an exciting venture into a daunting ordeal. They obsess over every technical detail, agonizing over microphone specs and editing software. Hours are spent tweaking audio levels and researching the perfect intro music. Meanwhile, the actual content of their show takes a backseat.

These would-be podcasters often fail to plan their content effectively. They might have a vague idea of what they want to discuss but no clear structure or long-term vision. They wing it episode by episode, hoping inspiration will strike when they hit the record button.

Here's the problem: this approach doesn't work. It's a recipe for burnout and inconsistent publishing. It's hard to stick to a publishing schedule when you are always fighting technical issues or scrambling for content ideas. Your listeners never know when to expect new episodes, making it challenging to build a loyal following.

Getting bogged down in technical details often results in poor audio quality and a subpar listener experience. Obsessing over the perfect sound can be a trap. It leads to endless tinkering and second-guessing. The result? Recordings that never meet your impossibly high standards.

Perhaps most importantly, this approach fails to build a loyal audience. Without consistent, engaging content, listeners have no reason to stick around. They might tune in for an episode or two, but they won't become the dedicated fans you're hoping for.

So, what should you do instead? The key is to simplify the podcasting process. Strip it down to its essentials. Focus on what matters: create high-quality, consistent content that resonates with your audience.

Instead of getting lost in technical minutiae, develop a clear, compelling voice for your show. Plan your content in advance, creating a roadmap for future episodes that aligns with your overall goals.

Your listeners want your insights, personality, and value. They don't care about perfect audio or fancy production tricks. It's vital to make your show sound professional. But, don't let tech issues overshadow your podcast's heart: the content.

Finally, strategies for audience growth should be implemented from day one. Don't obsess over download numbers. Focus on making a show that truly serves your listeners. Engage your audience. Encourage feedback. Refine your approach based on what resonates with them.

Simplify your process. Focus on content. Keep your audience in mind. Do this, and you'll build a successful podcast with a loyal, engaged audience.

Your Podcast Playbook: 7 Steps to Audio Stardom

Step 1: Choose Your Podcast's Home Base

Choosing a podcast host is like selecting a home base for your audio content. It's where your episodes will live and be distributed worldwide. You want a host that's reliable, easy to use, and capable of getting your show onto all the major podcast platforms.

For beginners, BuzzSprout stands out as a user-friendly option. It's like the Swiss Army knife of podcast hosting—simple enough for newbies but packed with features to grow with them. With BuzzSprout, you can upload your audio files, fill out your show details, and hit publish, all without breaking a sweat.

Remember, your hosting platform is the foundation of your podcast. Choose wisely, and you'll set yourself up for smooth sailing as your show grows.

Step 2: Map Out Your Content Journey

"If you fail to plan, you plan to fail." This old adage rings especially true in podcasting. As Joe Rogan, a top podcaster, puts it, "The key is to prepare as much as you can, but be willing to throw it all away and go with the flow."

Start by nailing down your core topic. What unique perspective can you bring to the table? Then, decide on your episode format. Will you do solo shows, interviews, or a mix of both? Finally, create a content calendar. Plan out your episodes in advance, ensuring a steady stream of engaging content.

Consistency and quality are the dynamic duo of podcast success. By planning ahead, you'll ensure you always have something valuable to share with your audience, keeping them coming back for more.

Step 3: Bring Your Voice to Life

On Christmas Eve, 1906, Reginald Fessenden made history. He conducted the first radio broadcast, reading Bible verses and playing "O Holy Night" on his violin. Expecting the Morse code, listeners on ships at sea were astonished to hear a human voice coming through their receivers.

Your first podcast episode may not make history. But, the principle remains: create clear, engaging audio content that will captivate your listeners.

Invest in a decent microphone and find a quiet space to record. But don't get bogged down in technical perfection. Remember, content is king. Your listeners are tuning in for your ideas and personality, not studio-quality audio.

Step 4: Craft Your Show's Digital Storefront

Think of your show notes and metadata as your podcast's digital storefront. They're what potential listeners see when browsing podcast directories. A study from the University of Texas found that podcasts with good, keyword-rich show notes saw a 35% rise in new listeners. This was compared to those with minimal descriptions.

Write compelling episode titles and descriptions. Include relevant keywords to boost your SEO. Add timestamps for key discussion points, making it easy for listeners to navigate your content.

Good show notes help new listeners find you. They also improve the experience for your current audience. They add value and boost engagement.

Step 5: Make a Grand Entrance

Launching a podcast is like opening a new restaurant. You wouldn't open your doors with just one dish on the menu, would you? Similarly, don't launch your podcast with just a single episode.

Aim to have 3-5 episodes ready at launch. This allows new listeners to binge and get hooked on your content. It also raises your chances of landing in Apple Podcasts' "New & Noteworthy" section. That can greatly boost your show's visibility.

Remember, first impressions count. Make sure your launch lineup showcases the best of what your podcast has to offer.

Step 6: Embrace the Power of Batching

"Never touch paper twice." Popularized by productivity expert David Allen, this principle applies beautifully to podcasting. Instead of scrambling to produce episodes week by week, try batch recording.

Set aside one day a month to record multiple episodes. This approach allows you to get into a flow state, resulting in more consistent, higher-quality content. It also gives you a buffer, reducing stress and ensuring you always have content ready to go.

By batching your podcast production, you'll free up time and mental energy to focus on growing your audience and improving your craft.

Step 7: Turn Listeners into Subscribers

Your podcast is more than just a content platform - it's a powerful tool for growing your email list. Take inspiration from John Lee Dumas, host of Entrepreneurs on Fire. By promoting a lead magnet at the start and end of each episode, he grew his email list from zero to over 100,000 subscribers in two years.

Create a lead magnet that provides additional value related to your podcast content. It could be a checklist, an ebook, or exclusive bonus content. Promote it consistently in your episodes, making it easy for listeners to access.

Turning listeners into email subscribers creates a direct link to your audience. It helps you build relationships, promote content, and grow your business.

Today's Exercise: Your Podcast Launch Blueprint

Let's map out the core elements of your podcast launch. This exercise will help you clarify your concept, plan content, and consider the practical aspects of creating your show. Remember, the goal isn't perfection – it's to get you started and build momentum.

Step 1. Podcast Concept

Begin by defining your podcast concept. Write down your podcast name and craft a single sentence that describes what your podcast is about. This will serve as your show's mission statement. Next, list three key topics you plan to cover in your episodes. This will help you stay focused and give potential listeners a clear idea of what to expect.

Step 2. Your First Three Episodes

Now, let's plan your first three episodes. Quickly outline each topic and jot down two or three key points you want to cover. This initial content plan will give you a solid starting point and help you avoid the blank-page syndrome when it's time to record.

Step 3. Your Tech Setup

Consider your technical setup. Choose a podcast hosting platform that fits your needs and budget. Choose your recording equipment. It could be as simple as your computer's built-in mic or as advanced as a dedicated podcast mic. Remember, you can always upgrade your equipment as your podcast grows.

Step 4. Your Recording Schedule

Establishing a recording schedule is crucial for consistency. Pick a date to record your first episode, and choose a regular recording day and time for future episodes. This routine will help you stay on track and give your listeners a reliable schedule to look forward to.

Step 5. Your Podcast Launch Promotion

Finally, think about how you'll promote your podcast launch. List three ways you'll spread the word – this could include leveraging social media, your email list, or your personal network. Write a short, engaging blurb of 2-3 sentences for your launch. Use it across platforms to generate buzz.

Once you've completed these steps, review what you've written. You now have a basic blueprint for your podcast launch. You've taken concrete steps towards turning your podcast idea into reality. Remember, you can continually refine these ideas later. The important thing is that you've begun the journey of launching your podcast!

Key Takeaways:

- Simplify your podcasting process with user-friendly tools and consistent practices.

- Launch strategically with multiple episodes and optimize for discoverability.

- Use your podcast to grow your email list by promoting your lead magnet.

13

The YouTube Traffic Playbook

A cheap camcorder. Zero training. A small church near Seattle. That's where Sean Cannell's journey began in 2003. No fancy equipment, no film school degree - just a spark of passion and a willingness to learn. Sean dove headfirst into video creation, armed with nothing but determination and a basic Adobe Premier setup. He cranked out 52 videos a year, building his "content creation muscle" one project at a time.

Fast-forward to today. Sean is the mastermind behind Think Media, a YouTube powerhouse with millions of subscribers. His company is raking in eight figures, and he's living proof that YouTube success isn't just a pipe dream.

But hold up. It wasn't all smooth sailing.

Sean faced his fair share of bumps along the way. His wife's health crisis nearly derailed everything, and he lost all his freelance clients in one brutal swoop. Yet he kept pushing, churning out content like a machine—at one point, he was talking 52 videos in just two months.[10]

Why does Sean's story matter to you?

It shows what's possible with grit, consistency, and a will to adapt. So, Sean didn't wait for the perfect moment or skills. He started scared, learned on the job, and kept showing up - even when life threw curveballs.

This chapter will explore strategies to grow YouTube channels into successful businesses. We'll unpack the techniques that helped Sean and countless others build their online empires.

Buckle up whether you're just starting out or looking to level up your existing channel. We're about to explore the wild, wonderful world of growing an audience on YouTube. Ready to turn your passion into a platform? Let's dive in.

The YouTube Trap

Most aspiring YouTubers fall into a common trap. They upload whatever strikes their fancy whenever they feel like it. There is no strategy or plan—just random content thrown at the wall, hoping something sticks.

They treat SEO as optional, ignoring the power of well-crafted titles, descriptions, and tags. Audience engagement is an afterthought, if it happens at all.

Here's the harsh truth: this approach is a one-way ticket to YouTube obscurity.

Without a clear focus, your channel becomes a confusing mess. Viewers can't figure out what you're about, so they don't stick around. Your videos get lost in the vast sea of content because you've ignored the very algorithm designed to help people find you.

And that inconsistency is killing your growth. Viewers crave reliability, and when you don't deliver, they move on to channels that will.

So, what's the alternative?

It's time to flip the script.

Start with a rock-solid content strategy. Know your niche, understand your audience, and plan your videos with purpose.

Embrace SEO like it's your new best friend. Learn the ins and outs of YouTube's algorithm and make it work for you, not against you.

And here's the real game-changer: engage with your audience like your channel depends on it - because it does. Respond to comments, ask for feedback, and analyze your performance data like a pro.

Remember, growing on YouTube isn't about luck. It's about strategy, optimization, and consistent engagement. Master these, and you'll be light-years ahead of the competition.

The YouTube Growth Playbook

Most YouTubers are playing a losing game. They upload random videos, ignore SEO, and treat audience engagement as an afterthought. It's like throwing darts blindfolded and hoping to hit the bullseye.

This scattershot approach leads nowhere fast. Viewers get confused by the lack of focus; your videos get buried by YouTube's algorithm, and your growth stalls. It's a recipe for frustration and burnout.

So, what's the winning strategy?

First, ditch the randomness. Develop a clear content strategy that speaks to your audience's needs and interests. Then, make YouTube's algorithm your ally, not your enemy. Finally, engage with your viewers like your channel's life depends on it - because it does.

Ready to level up? Here's your step-by-step guide:

1. Master Keyword Research

Don't guess what topics will resonate. Use tools like TubeBuddy or VidIQ to find popular, low-competition keywords. It's like having a treasure map for your niche. Choosing YouTube topics without keyword research is like fishing without knowing where the fish are.

2. Craft Compelling Content

Focus on one of three video styles: Talking Head, Presentation Slides, or Screenshare Recording. Whichever you choose, make it engaging. As Gary Vaynerchuk says, "Content is king, but engagement is the kingdom."

3. Optimize for SEO

Craft titles, descriptions, and tags that sing to both viewers and YouTube's algorithm. Think of SEO as putting up clear road signs to your content in a busy city of videos. Make it easy for your audience to find you.

4. Create Thumb-Stopping Thumbnails

Your thumbnail is your video's movie poster. Make it pop! Use tools like Canva to create visuals that demand attention. As YouTube expert Roberto Blake advises, "Your thumbnail is your video's movie poster. Make it pop!"

5. Publish Consistently

Establish a regular publishing schedule. Treat it like watering a plant - it's essential for growth. Consider using YouTube Shorts. They can diversify your content and reach new audiences.

By following these steps, you'll transform your YouTube strategy from haphazard to laser-focused. You'll work smarter, not harder, and watch your audience grow. Remember, success on YouTube isn't about luck - it's about strategy, optimization, and consistent effort.

Advanced YouTube Strategies: Taking Your Channel to the Next Level

Ready to supercharge your YouTube growth? Let's dive into some advanced strategies that can set you apart from the crowd.

Double Your Visibility with Google Search

Want to cast a wider net? Look for keywords in your niche that display videos in Google search results. This clever tactic puts your content in front of viewers on both YouTube and Google.

"Visibility is the key to success," says one digital marketing expert. "When your video appears in both YouTube and Google search results, you're essentially fishing in two ponds with one line."

Imagine doubling your reach with the same amount of effort. That's the power of this strategy.

Harness Your Email List for Instant Momentum

Have an email list? Use it to boost your new videos. Send out an email within 24 hours of publishing. This initial surge of views tells YouTube your content is worth showing to more people.

Think of your email list as your loyal fan club. When you release a new video, they're the first ones to cheer you on, giving you the momentum to reach a wider audience.

Tap into YouTube's Brain

Have you ever wished you could peek inside YouTube's mind? Now you can. Head to the Inspiration tab in YouTube Studio. It's a goldmine of personalized insights:

- "What people are looking for": Trending keyword phrases

- "New videos to inspire you": Successful competitor videos

- "Make a short": Topic suggestions for YouTube Shorts

As one YouTube strategy consultant says, "The Inspiration tab is like having a direct line to YouTube's brain. It tells you exactly what the platform and its users are hungry for."

Become a Content Detective

It's time to put on your detective hat and analyze your more successful competitors' channels. What are their most popular videos? Which recent uploads are outperforming the rest?

Use these insights to inform your content strategy. But remember, you're not copying - you're finding inspiration.

One expert explains, "Studying your competitors is like being a detective in the world of content creation. You're looking for clues about what resonates with your shared audience, then using that information to craft your own unique approach."

By implementing these advanced strategies, you're not just playing the YouTube game but changing it. You're finding hidden opportunities, using your assets, and outpacing the competition.

Remember, success on YouTube isn't just about creating great content. It's about being innovative, strategic, and always looking for new ways to grow. So go ahead and give these tactics a try. Your future YouTube stardom awaits!

Today's Exercise: YouTube Topic Brainstorm Exercise

Ready to uncover your next viral video idea? Let's flex those creative muscles with this YouTube topic brainstorming exercise. Grab a pen and paper - it's time to dive in!

1. Core Interests Dump: Write down everything you're passionate about. Don't overthink it. Hobbies, skills, experiences - jot it all down.

2. Audience Pain Points: For each interest, list potential problems or questions your audience might have. What keeps them up at night?

3. Keyword Exploration: Use YouTube's search bar. Type in your topics and see what auto-completes. These are golden nuggets of viewer interest.

4. Trend Surfing: Check Google Trends or YouTube Trending. Can you put your unique spin on a hot topic?

5. Question Overload: Write down as many questions as possible about your top 3 interests. What, why, how, when - get curious!

6. Title Tease: Craft 5 attention-grabbing titles for your top ideas. Remember, intrigue sells!

7. Gut Check: Circle your top 3 ideas. Which ones excite you most? Which could provide the most value to your audience?

Congratulations! You've just generated a goldmine of video ideas tailored to your passions and your audience's needs. Pick your favorite and start planning that video. Remember, the best idea is the one you actually create. So, what are you waiting for? Lights, camera, action!

Key Takeaways:

- Keyword research and SEO are vital for growth on YouTube.

- Consistent, high-quality content creation in a recognizable style helps build a loyal audience.

- Engaging with your audience and analyzing performance data are key to long-term success on the platform.

14

The Pinterest Traffic Playbook

I t's early 2020, and the Pinterest world is suddenly in chaos. Bloggers and content creators with successful businesses on the platform are watching their traffic plummet overnight. Panic spreads like wildfire in online communities. People frantically try to find out what's gone wrong. Welcome to "Repin-Gate" - the great Pinterest panic of 2020.

Overnight, the rules of the game changed. Pinterest's algorithm, once a reliable friend to content creators, seemed to turn against them. Repins, once the lifeblood of Pinterest's strategy, were suddenly toxic. Fresh content became king, but what exactly did that mean? The digital world was changing fast. Many wondered if Pinterest was still a good traffic source.

But here's the thing: while some threw in the towel, others saw an opportunity. They realized this seismic shift wasn't the death knell for Pinterest traffic but a chance to soar above the competition. These savvy creators decoded the new algorithm. They crafted strategies that recovered and boosted their lost traffic.[11]

That's precisely what we're going to explore in this chapter. We'll uncover the secrets of Pinterest's new algorithm. We'll debunk outdated advice that's still around. Finally, we'll give you a step-by-step system to harness Pinterest's traffic that works today.

This chapter will help you, whether you're a Pinterest newbie or a pro shaken by recent changes. It will give you the knowledge and strategies you need. You'll learn to create "fresh" content that Pinterest loves. You'll also learn to leverage third-party pins and optimize your profile for visibility.

By the end of this chapter, you'll have a clear roadmap for turning Pinterest into a reliable, powerful traffic source for your website or blog. So, let's dive in and unlock the secrets of Pinterest traffic in the post-Repin-Gate era.

Pinterest Pitfalls and Power Moves

Why Pinterest? Many digital marketers and content creators grapple with this, especially in a world dominated by flashy social media. But, savvy marketers know a secret: Pinterest isn't just a social media site. It's a powerful visual search engine. It can drive targeted traffic to your site.

While many mistake Pinterest for just another social network, its true power lies in its search functionality. Unlike other platforms, Pinterest pins last. They can drive traffic for months or even years after posting. It's a platform where users search for ideas, products, and solutions. It's a goldmine for businesses and creators who can use it well.

This is where Pinterest SEO comes into play. Just as you'd optimize your website for Google, do the same for Pinterest. It can greatly boost your visibility and reach. By using Pinterest SEO strategies, you're not just throwing content into the void. You're positioning yourself to be found by users seeking what you offer. Mastering Pinterest SEO is a must. It's the key to its true power as a traffic-driving powerhouse.

Before we discuss what works, let's address the elephant in the room: the common mistakes that many Pinterest users still make. These missteps can sabotage your efforts before you even get started.

Relying too heavily on repins

Remember when repinning was the holy grail of Pinterest strategy? Those days are long gone. Many users still cling to the outdated belief that repinning their content across multiple boards is the key to success. This approach can now harm your account, triggering Pinterest's spam filters and reducing your overall reach.

Ignoring third-party content

Some users have overreacted to the algorithm changes. They have now abandoned all third-party content. This is like trying to build a thriving community by talking only to yourself. Pinterest no longer requires you to pin others' content. But, adding some high-quality third-party pins can boost your content's visibility.

Focusing solely on creating new pins

Creating fresh content is crucial, but some users have interpreted this to mean they must churn out dozens of new pins daily. This approach often leads to burnout and a decrease in pin quality. Quality trumps quantity in the new Pinterest landscape.

The New Rules of Pinterest Traffic

Now that we've clarified what not to do let's focus on the new rules governing Pinterest traffic.

Fresh content doesn't necessarily mean brand-new blog posts or products. Pinterest defines fresh content as new pin images, even if they link to existing content on your site. Creating new pin designs allows you to breathe new life into old blog posts. It's not about reinventing the wheel but rather presenting it in fresh, engaging ways.

In the race to create fresh content, quality often takes a backseat. However, Pinterest's algorithm is sophisticated enough to recognize and prioritize high-quality pins. This means clear, visually appealing images, compelling titles, and value-added descriptions. Think of each pin as a mini-billboard for your content – it needs to stop scrollers in their tracks and compel them to click.

Pinterest no longer requires sharing others' content. But, using high-quality third-party pins can boost your account's performance. It's all about creating a rich, diverse Pinterest presence that provides value to your followers beyond just your own content. Think of it as curating an engaging, varied museum exhibit rather than a one-artist show.

By understanding and applying these new rules, you're setting the stage for Pinterest's success. In the next section, we'll explain how to implement these principles in a step-by-step guide to mastering Pinterest traffic.

Pinterest Success Blueprint: Your Step-by-Step Guide

Now that we've addressed common mistakes and new rules, it's time to roll up our sleeves and get to work. Let's explore your roadmap to Pinterest success in five actionable steps.

Step 1: Optimize Your Pinterest Profile

Begin by choosing a clear, keyword-rich username representing your brand or niche. Craft an engaging bio that introduces you and incorporates your niche and target keywords. Use a high-quality profile picture. Use your business logo or a professional headshot for personal brands. Create board covers that align with your brand aesthetic to give your profile a cohesive and professional look.

Think of your Pinterest profile as a storefront on a bustling digital street. Like a great shop window, an optimized Pinterest profile attracts passersby. It entices them to follow and buy. Your username is your store sign, your bio is the window display, and your boards are the carefully curated product sections. Make each element count.

Your profile is your first impression. To attract your ideal audience, make it clear, professional, and aligned with your brand.

Step 2: Create "Fresh" Content Consistently

Aim to create 5-10 fresh pins daily to keep your content stream active. Vary your pin designs while maintaining brand consistency to keep your audience engaged. Repurpose existing content. Create new images and descriptions. This will maximize your content's reach. Consider using a scheduling tool to maintain consistency without burning out.

A 2022 study from the University of Texas found that websites updating content at least three times a week saw a 50% increase in organic traffic. This was compared to sites that updated less often. The same principle applies to Pinterest. Fresh content signals to the algorithm that your account is active and valuable.

Consistency is king. Regular, fresh content keeps your account visible and engaging to the Pinterest algorithm and your audience.

Step 3: Leverage Third-Party Content Strategically

Save high-ranking pins in your niche to relevant boards to boost your account's overall relevance. Pin directly from websites, not repins on Pinterest. This will diversify your content. Use third-party content to "prime" seasonal boards. Then, add your own content to create a better resource for your followers. Aim to maintain a ratio of about 80% of your content to 20% of third-party content.

In nature, symbiotic relationships benefit all parties involved. Similarly, strategically incorporating third-party content can boost your own pins' visibility. It's about creating a rich, diverse Pinterest ecosystem that provides value beyond just your own content.

Third-party content isn't your enemy – it's a powerful ally when used strategically.

Step 4: Master Pinterest SEO

Use keyword-rich titles and descriptions for your pins and boards to improve searchability. Incorporate relevant keywords naturally into your pin text overlays to enhance their discoverability. Create board titles that align with common search terms in your niche to attract your target audience. Utilize Pinterest's guided search feature to discover popular keywords and stay on top of trending topics.

"Pinterest is a search engine first, social media platform second. Treat it as such, and you'll see your traffic soar," says Pinterest expert Kate Ahl of Simple Pin Media. This quote underscores the critical importance of SEO on Pinterest.

SEO isn't just for Google. Mastering Pinterest SEO can dramatically increase your content's discoverability.

Step 5: Engage with the Pinterest Community

Reply to comments on your pins. This builds community and encourages more engagement. Join and participate in relevant group boards to expand your reach and connect with like-minded creators. Collaborate with other creators in your niche to cross-pollinate audiences and gain new followers. Use Pinterest's native features, like Story Pins, to boost engagement and show your personality.

Consider the story of food blogger Sally McKenney. After she engaged with her Pinterest community, her pageviews soared. They jumped from 50,000 to over 5 million in 18 months. She did this by responding to comments, joining group boards, and collaborating with fellow food bloggers.

Pinterest isn't just a place to post content – it's a community. Engage with that community to build relationships and boost your visibility.

By following these five steps consistently, you'll be well on your way to Pinterest success. Stay patient, stay consistent, and watch your traffic grow.

Today's Exercise: Today's Pinterest Quick-Win Exercise

Let's supercharge your Pinterest presence with a few simple actions you can complete today. This exercise is designed to boost your account immediately without overwhelming you. Feel free to tackle these tasks at your own pace – the goal is to complete them by the end of the day.

1. Keyword Discovery

Go to Pinterest and type in your main niche topic. Write down the first 5-10 suggested search terms that appear. These are golden nuggets for your Pinterest strategy.

2. Fresh Pin Creation

Choose one of your most popular blog posts or products. Using Canva or your preferred design tool, create a new pin image for it. Incorporate one of the keywords you just discovered into the pin's text overlay. This fresh content will signal to Pinterest that your account is active and valuable.

3. Strategic Third-Party Pin

Search for a high-performing pin in your niche using one of your newly found keywords. Save this pin to one of your relevant boards. Remember to save directly from the source website, not from within Pinterest. This action helps build connections between your content and popular pins in your niche.

4. Optimize an Existing Pin

Select one of your existing pins and give its description a makeover. Rewrite it, naturally incorporating 2-3 of your newly found keywords. This simple update can breathe new life into older content.

5. Quick Engagement

Find and comment on 2-3 pins in your niche. Make your comments thoughtful and add value to the conversation. This small act of engagement can increase your visibility within the Pinterest community.

Completing these tasks will help you improve your Pinterest presence. You've optimized for keywords, created new content, engaged with your community, and used third-party content. All are key to a successful Pinterest strategy.

Remember, consistency is key on Pinterest. Try to incorporate similar optimization activities into your routine regularly. Even small, consistent efforts can significantly improve your Pinterest performance over time.

Key Takeaways:

- Pinterest is still a valuable traffic source when used correctly.

- Focus on consistently creating fresh, high-quality content.

- Balance your own content with strategic use of third-party pins.

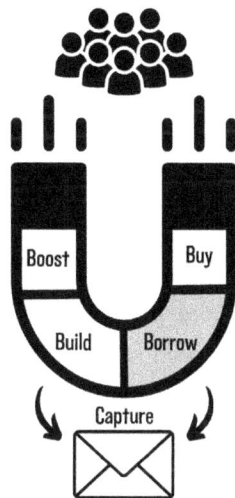

The Borrow Method
(Partner Traffic)

15

The Guest Blogging Traffic Playbook

T heir book was rejected by 144 publishers, sales flatlined, and two authors were on the brink of giving up. This was the reality for Jack Canfield and Mark Victor Hansen when they launched "Chicken Soup for the Soul" in 1993.

Fast forward a couple of years. The same book is a bestseller. It is flying off shelves and is spawning a multi-million dollar franchise. What changed?

The secret ingredient? Media mentions.

Canfield and Hansen didn't just sit back and hope for the best. They cooked up a media storm. They pitched themselves to radio shows, TV programs, and newspapers. Big or small, it didn't matter. They were everywhere.

Have you heard of the Rule of Five? That's what they called their strategy. Every single day, they'd do five things to promote their book: five calls, five emails, five interviews—whatever it took to get people talking.

And boy, did people talk.

One appearance on Oprah. Boom. Millions of viewers suddenly crave their book.

Even a shoutout from country star Naomi Judd sent sales soaring.

Each mention was a stepping stone, each interview a building block. Before long, "Chicken Soup for the Soul" wasn't just a book—it was a phenomenon.[12]

Here's the kicker: They didn't have a massive marketing budget. No fancy PR team. Just two guys with a book and a whole lot of determination.

So, what's the takeaway?

Media mentions aren't just nice to have. They're the secret sauce that can turn your brand from zero to hero. And the best part? You don't need to be a household name to make it happen.

Ready to write your own success story? Let's learn how to create a media mention strategy that will have your brand sizzling in no time.

The Guest Blogging Grind

Ever feel like you're shouting into the void? That's what most people's guest blogging strategy looks like. The typical playbook involves sending countless cold emails to any blog that will listen. Then, you cross your fingers and hope someone bites. You spend hours crafting the perfect SEO-optimized post, tack on a bio with your precious backlink, submit it, and pray they like it. Then comes the endless cycle of following up again and again. It's exhausting just thinking about it.

Why It's a Dead End

Let's face it. This approach is about as practical as trying to fill a swimming pool with a teaspoon. It's a massive time sink, with hours upon hours spent on a single link that might not even see the light of day. You're at the mercy of other people's schedules, never knowing when or if your post will be published. The payoff is uncertain at best - will it drive traffic? Boost your rankings? Who knows? It's like playing darts blindfolded. You might hit the bullseye, but odds are you'll just end up with a lot of holes in the wall.

A Smarter Way: Media Mentions

What if there was a way to get more bang for your buck? Enter media mentions. Instead of chasing after every blog under the sun, why not tap into platforms that already have massive audiences? This approach works because you're piggybacking on established credibility. When a big-name outlet mentions you, people listen. High-traffic sites mean more eyeballs on your brand - it's simple math. Quality trumps quantity here. One mention from a reputable source can outweigh dozens of guest posts on unknown blogs.

Think about it. Would you rather have a whisper heard by a few or a shoutout on a megaphone? Media mentions are your ticket to the big leagues. They're your shortcut to reaching thousands, even millions, of potential readers. And the best part? You don't have to write a novel to make it happen.

Ready to ditch the guest post hamster wheel and start playing in the big leagues? Let's dive into how you can make media mentions work for you. This could revolutionize your outreach. It would save you time and boost your visibility. It's time to stop shouting into the void. We must connect with our target audience through strategic media mentions.

Your Media Mentions Playbook

Ready to make waves? Let's break down the process step by step.

1. Tap into HARO

HARO stands for Help a Reporter Out. It's your golden ticket to media mentions. Sign up for free, and you'll get daily emails packed with journalistic queries. It's like a matchmaking service for experts and journalists. You provide the know-how; they provide the platform.

2. Cherry-pick Your Queries

Don't spread yourself thin. Focus on queries that align with your expertise and target audience. As Gary Keller said, "The key is not to do more things but to focus on the right things." Be selective. Quality trumps quantity every time.

3. Craft Snappy Responses

Journalists are busy. Make their job easy. Keep your responses under 150 words. Pack them with clear, quotable insights. Think of it like a Twitter thread – concise yet impactful. Get to the point fast and make every word count.

4. Polish Your Bio

Your bio is your handshake. Keep it short and relevant, and include a link to your blog. Remember Ann Handley's wisdom: "Your bio is not a resume; it's a handshake." Make it warm, professional, and memorable.

5. Play the Numbers Game

Increase your odds by responding to multiple queries daily. It's like playing the lottery but with skills instead of luck. The more quality responses you submit, the higher your chances of getting picked up.

6. Track and Follow Up

Keep tabs on your submissions. Create a simple spreadsheet to log your responses. Follow up on potential publications. Remember, "The fortune is in the follow-up," as Jim Rohn put it. Don't let opportunities slip through the cracks.

7. Amplify Your Mentions

When you score a mention, don't just sit on it. Share it. Promote it across your platforms. Each media mention is a seed. Nurture it to grow your audience. Post it on social media, feature it on your website, and include it in your email newsletter.

This strategy isn't about overnight success. It's about consistent, focused effort. Each step builds on the last, creating a snowball effect of credibility and visibility.

Remember, every major brand started somewhere. Your next HARO response could be the first step towards becoming a recognized expert in your field. So, ready to dive in?

Today's Exercise: Submit Your First HARO Response

Here's a practical exercise to get you started on your media mentions journey. Set aside a couple of hours, and let's make some magic happen.

First, head to HARO's website and sign up for a free account. It's quick, easy, and won't cost you a dime.

Once you're in, check your inbox for the day's HARO email. It's a treasure trove of opportunities. Scan through the queries and pick 3-5 that align with your expertise. Don't bite off more than you can chew – quality matters.

Now, roll up your sleeves and craft your responses. Remember, keep them under 150 words. Be clear, concise, and quotable. Imagine you're explaining your point to a friend over coffee.

Next, write a short, snappy bio—two or three sentences max. Highlight your expertise and include a link to your blog. Make it impossible for them not to want to know more about you.

It's time to hit send. Submit your responses through the HARO platform. Take a deep breath—you're putting yourself out there, and that's huge.

Don't let your hard work go to waste. Set up a simple spreadsheet to track your submissions. Include the query details and submission dates. This will be your roadmap moving forward.

As the day wraps up, take a moment to reflect. How did it feel? What could you do better tomorrow? Commit to making this a daily habit.

Remember, consistency is key. Rome wasn't built in a day, and neither is media presence. But with each query you answer, you're one step closer to becoming a go-to expert in your field.

So, what are you waiting for? Your first media mention could be just a HARO response away. Let's get cracking!

Key Takeaways:

- Efficiency is key. Focus on high-impact strategies, like media mentions, over time-consuming guest posts.

- Leverage existing platforms: Use HARO to connect with top media outlets and get valuable backlinks.

- Consistency matters. Regular, expert insights can boost audience growth and SEO.

16

The Guest Podcasting Traffic Playbook

My book publisher set the launch date for my new book, "Your Message Matters," for October 2020, right in the middle of the global pandemic. This date had been established 18 months prior. No one could predict what the future would hold.

The challenge? My primary strategy to promote the book was attending conferences and events. Speaking gigs were going to be my ticket to visibility. But with the pandemic, everything changed.

Then, one day, I had an idea. What if I solely focused on getting on 100 or more podcasts? This way, I could still leverage speaking and promote my book by getting in front of new audiences weekly.

For the next 18 months, I did precisely that. Rarely did a week pass without a podcast interview lined up. Most weeks, I'd have two or three.

Today, I call this my hidden stages strategy. Each podcast has an audience of people already gathered around a shared topic they're passionate about. If your message aligns with these audiences, why not get in front of them through guest podcasting?

It's a great way to be featured as an expert. And here's the kicker - you don't need a book to use this strategy. Guest podcasting can be your secret weapon for building your audience and spreading your message.

In this chapter, we'll dive into the Guest Podcasting Playbook. You'll learn how to turn podcast appearances into powerful platforms for your ideas. Ready to step onto these hidden stages? Let's get started.

The Podcast Guest Pitfall: Common Mistakes and Smarter Strategies

Most people dive into guest podcasting with high hopes and little strategy. They fire off cold emails to big-name podcasts, dreaming of instant exposure. The hours tick by as they craft pitch after pitch, only to hear crickets in response. Frustration sets in. The process of landing even one interview feels like pulling teeth.

Others take the opposite approach. They jump at any opportunity, no matter how small. They end up on brand-new podcasts with barely any listeners. Sure, they get to speak, but to whom? The host's mom and maybe a handful of others. The result? It wasted time and had minimal impact.

Here's the hard truth: popular podcasts are drowning in guest requests. Your carefully crafted email? It's likely lost in a sea of similar pitches. Standing out feels nearly impossible.

On the flip side, new podcasts might welcome you with open arms. But they lack what you need most: an established audience. You're essentially shouting your message into the void.

Both paths lead to the same dead end. You invest heaps of time with little to show for it. It's a recipe for burnout and disappointment.

Your Guest Podcasting Game: A Better Approach

There's a smarter way to play the guest podcasting game. Enter podcast matching services. These platforms quickly connect you to relevant shows. No more random emails or settling for shows with no listeners.

Focus your energy on shows with established, engaged audiences in your niche. These are the hidden gems that can truly amplify your message.

Develop a system for your guest podcasting efforts. Treat it like a professional campaign, not a haphazard hobby. With the right approach, you'll turn podcast appearances into powerful platforms for your ideas.

Ready to revolutionize your guest podcasting strategy? Let's explore the steps that will set you apart from the crowd.

7 Steps to Master Guest Podcasting

Stop wasting time with cold emails. Sign up for services like Pod-Match to connect with suitable podcast hosts. These platforms are game-changers. They use intelligent algorithms to match you with shows that align with your expertise.

Create a comprehensive profile that showcases your expertise and message. Think of PodMatch as a dating app for podcast hosts and guests. It helps you find your perfect match in the podcasting world. The more detailed your profile, the better your matches will be.

Optimize Your Guest Profile

Your profile is your podcast resume. Make it shine to attract the right opportunities. Craft a compelling bio that highlights your unique value proposition. What makes you different? Why should hosts want you on their show?

Don't forget to include relevant links, social media profiles, and previous podcast appearances. These provide social proof and give hosts a taste of your style. A well-crafted profile can open doors you didn't even know existed.

Tailor Your Pitch

Research each podcast before reaching out. Listen to a few episodes. Get a feel for the host's style and the show's content. This knowledge is your secret weapon.

Customize your pitch to align with the show's content and audience. Generic pitches scream, "Delete me." Tailored pitches show you care. Pitching to a podcast is like applying for a job. Tailor your application to stand out from the crowd.

Prepare Engaging Content

Develop a repertoire of interesting stories, case studies, and action-able advice. These are your go-to content pieces. They should be relevant, engaging, and adaptable to different shows.

Create a one-sheet with potential discussion topics and key talking points. This isn't just for the host - it's for you, too. Preparation is the key to confidence. The more prepared you are, the more value you can provide to the audience.

Deliver Value During the Interview

Focus on providing actionable insights and entertainment for the audience. They're tuning in to learn something new or to be inspired. Don't disappoint them.

Share personal anecdotes to make your message more relatable. Stories stick in people's minds long after facts fade. Think of each podcast interview as a mini TED Talk - inform, inspire, and leave the audience wanting more.

Promote Your Appearances

Your job isn't done when the interview ends. Share your podcast appearances across your social media channels and let your network know about your latest guest spot.

Create content around each interview. Write blog posts expanding on topics you discussed. Share snippets on social media. Each podcast appearance is a seed. Nurture it through promotion to help it grow into new opportunities.

Follow Up and Build Relationships

Send thank-you notes to hosts after each interview. A little gratitude goes a long way, and it sets you apart from other guests who disappear after the recording stops.

Stay in touch with hosts for potential future collaborations. Guest podcasting is not just about one-time appearances. It's about cultivating a network of valuable relationships in your industry. These connections can lead to unexpected opportunities down the road.

Master these steps, and you'll transform from a podcast guest into a sought-after expert in your field. Are you ready to take the podcasting world by storm?

Today's Exercise: Your 24-Hour Guest Podcasting Launch

Ready to kickstart your guest podcasting journey? Let's turn theory into action with this one-day practical exercise. By the end of it, you'll have laid the groundwork for your first podcast appearances.

Start by signing up for a podcast matching service like PodMatch. This will be your launchpad for finding relevant shows. Once you're in, set a timer for 30 minutes and craft your guest profile. Focus on highlighting your expertise and unique value proposition. What makes you stand out? Why should hosts want you on their show?

Next, put on your detective hat. Spend an hour researching and identifying five podcasts in your niche that align with your message. Listen to snippets of their shows to get a feel for their style and audience.

Now comes the creative part. Draft a customized pitch for each of these five podcasts. Remember, one size doesn't fit all. Tailor each pitch to the specific show. This might take you about an hour, but it's time well spent.

Create a one-sheet document outlining 3-5 potential discussion topics related to your expertise. Think of this as your conversation menu. What juicy topics can you offer hosts to choose from?

It's time to polish your delivery. Spend 15 minutes practicing your key talking points. Aim for concise, engaging communication. Imagine you're explaining your ideas to a friend over coffee.

Finally, take a deep breath and hit send. Reach out to the five iden-
tified podcasts with your tailored pitches. You've done the groundwork. Now, it's time to put yourself out there.

By the end of this exercise, you'll have:

- A professional profile on a podcast-matching platform

- Five carefully researched podcast targets

- Five customized pitches

- A one-sheet of compelling discussion topics

- Practiced delivery of your key messages

Remember, this is just the beginning. Guest podcasting is a
marathon, not a sprint. But with this foundation, you're off to a
strong start. Ready to take the plunge?

Key Takeaways:

- Guest podcasting is a "hidden stages strategy." It can reach
  engaged audiences and promote your message. It's effective
  when traditional promotion methods are limited.

- Use podcast matching platforms. Optimize your guest profile. This will help you connect with relevant shows and
  stand out as a potential guest.

- To maximize your guest podcasting, focus on three things.
  First, deliver value in interviews. Second, promote your appearances. Third, build lasting relationships.

17

The Guest Video Traffic Playbook

I t was early 2015. I sat at my desk, staring at my goals for the year. One goal kept taunting me: host a virtual summit. For years, I'd watched others do it. They'd interview 10 to 20 experts on a hot topic, and boom - thousands of new email subscribers in days. It seemed like magic.

How did it work? Simple. Experts emailed their lists about the free summit. People signed up with their email to access the recordings—instant list growth.

I took a deep breath and decided: This was my year. I launched the Amplify Summit, focusing on writing, speaking, and coaching. I lined up 30 expert interviews. My heart raced as I hit "send" on the promotional emails.

Two weeks later, I blinked at my screen in disbelief—6,500 new subscribers. My list had exploded in growth.

That's the power of the guest interview strategy. But here's the kicker: You don't need to host a massive summit to win. Being a guest can be just as powerful.

Ready to supercharge your audience growth? Let's dive into the world of video interviews. You'll learn how to land coveted guest spots and host your own attention-grabbing events. Buckle up - your audience is about to get a whole lot bigger.

The Video Interview Strategy: Breaking Free from Obscurity

You've got valuable insights to share. But are you falling into common traps that keep you hidden from your ideal audience?

Let's talk about what doesn't work. Many creators sit back and wait for interview invitations to roll in. They believe their content will magically attract attention. Spoiler alert: It won't. When you're new, no one knows you exist. Your brilliance is trapped in a bubble of anonymity.

Even if you've started reaching out, inconsistent efforts lead nowhere. A few sporadic emails won't cut it. You need a system, not wishful thinking.

Why do these old-school approaches fail? They keep you small. Your potential audience never hears your voice. Your network grows at a snail's pace, if at all. Worst of all? You miss out on collaborative opportunities that could skyrocket your visibility.

It's time for a paradigm shift. Successful creators take control of their interview destiny. They don't wait to be chosen – they choose themselves.

Here's the secret: Become both the guest and the host. As a guest, you tap into established audiences. As a host, you build your own platform and attract high-level collaborators.

Technology is your ally in this new world. Virtual events have exploded, creating more opportunities than ever before. Online summit platforms, video tools, and social media make it easy to connect with potential partners and audiences.

The key is proactivity. Don't wait for permission. Seek out interview opportunities relentlessly. Create your own events to showcase your expertise alongside others in your field.

This dual approach isn't just about getting more eyeballs on your content. It's about quickly growing your network and credibility. It's about becoming a go-to expert in your niche.

Are you ready to step into the spotlight? Let's dive into the specific strategies that will transform you from unknown to in-demand.

Stepping into the Spotlight: Your Video Interview Action Plan

Ready to become the go-to expert in your field? Let's break down the steps to video interview success.

Step 1: Build Your Digital Stage

First, create a magnetic online presence. Register on speaker networks like heysummit.com. These platforms are your ticket to visibility.

Craft a speaker profile that sings. Highlight your unique expertise and the value you bring. Be specific about your availability for virtual events, in-person gigs, and podcast interviews.

Think of your profile as a 24/7 talent agent. It's always pitching you to potential hosts, even while you sleep.

Step 2: Become a Detective

It's time to get strategic. Use Google to your advantage. Search for "your topic + virtual summit" and uncover a goldmine of opportunities.

Reach out to past summit hosts. Ask about future events or if they know other organizers in your niche. Remember, every connection is a potential door to new audiences.

Step 3: Ride the Wave

Have you landed a high-profile interview? Fantastic. Now, milk it for all it's worth.

Share it everywhere. Your website, social media, email list – spread the word. One successful interview can snowball into an avalanche of opportunities.

Take my experience with John Lee Dumas on Entrepreneur on Fire. After that aired, I received daily interview requests for six months straight. That's the power of momentum.

Step 4: Become the Host

Ready to level up? Host your own virtual summit. Here's how:

- Pick a hot topic in your niche

- Set a date (give yourself at least 2-3 months of prep time)

- Dream big: List 30 potential guest experts

- Reach out and aim to confirm 10-15 participants

By hosting a summit, you're not just joining the conversation but leading it.

Step 5: Execute with Excellence

Now, bring your summit to life:

- Conduct engaging 30-minute interviews with each expert

- Set up a simple, compelling landing page for free registration

- Work with your guests to promote the summit to their audiences

Think of your summit as a potluck dinner party. Everyone brings a specialty dish (their expertise) and leaves satisfied (with new knowledge and connections).

Remember, each step builds on the last. As you gain experience and exposure, doors will open wider and faster. Stay consistent, stay curious, and watch your audience grow.

Your voice matters. It's time to amplify it through the power of video interviews.

Today's Exercise: Create Your Guest Expert One-Pager

Ready to position yourself as an irresistible interview guest? Let's build your one-pager. This powerful tool will make you stand out to potential hosts and streamline your outreach efforts.

1. Snap That Headshot

Get a professional-looking photo that shows your personality. Smile. Make eye contact with the camera. Use natural light if possible.Th ere is no need for a fancy studio— a simple, clean background works wonders.

2. Craft Your Bio

Write a punchy 2-3 sentence bio. Hook readers with your unique expertise or perspective. What makes you different? What results have you achieved for others? Keep it tight and compelling.

3. Identify Your Hot Topics

List 3-5 main topics you love discussing. Be specific. Instead of "marketing," try "Instagram reels for solopreneurs" or "Email sequences that convert cold leads."

4. Spark Conversation

Brainstorm 5-7 intriguing questions hosts could ask you. These should showcase your expertise and promise valuable insights for the audience. For example:

• "What's the biggest mistake you see new entrepreneurs make with [your topic]?"

• "Can you provide a case study of how you helped a client [achieve a specific result]?"

5. Showcase Your Style

Include links to 2-3 of your best previous interviews or talks. No prior interviews? Link to a blog post or video where you're sharing your expertise.

6. Make It Easy to Book You

Add your contact information and any relevant social media links. Include your time zone and general availability for interviews.

7. Register on HeySummit

Head to HeySummit.com and create your speaker profile. Use the elements you've just created to fill it out completely. This puts you on the radar of summit organizers looking for fresh voices.

Now, combine all these elements into a single, visually appealing document. Keep it to one page—hosts are busy and appreciate concise information.

Your Challenge: Spend the next hour creating your one-pager. Don't aim for perfection - done is better than perfect. You can always refine it later.

Remember, this one-pager is your ticket to more interviews and a broader audience. It's worth investing time to get it right. Once it's ready, you'll have a powerful tool to supercharge your outreach efforts.

Key Takeaways:

- Proactively seek interview opportunities via speaker networks and direct outreach to expand your audience.

- Use the momentum from high-profile interviews. Secure more guest spots to greatly boost your visibility.

- Hosting your own virtual summit can dramatically accelerate list growth and establish you as an authority in your niche.

18

The Guest Email Traffic Playbook

Meet Joseph Nicoletti, a former corporate worker who dared to dream big. By day, he punched the clock. By night, he hustled to build his online empire. Joseph's breakthrough came when he spotted a golden opportunity in the writing world.

Writers were struggling with Scrivener, a popular book-writing software. They'd buy it, then scratch their heads, wondering how to use it. Joseph saw their frustration and thought, "I can fix this!"

He rolled up his sleeves and created a step-by-step video course on mastering Scrivener. But here's the catch: Joseph had a solution but no audience. How could he reach the writers who needed his help?

That's when Joseph stumbled upon the magic of partner traffic. He asked himself, "Who already has the audience I want to reach?" Lightbulb moment!

Joseph reached out to influencers in the writing space. He offered to host free webinars for their audiences, teaching them Scrivener basics. Ultimately, he'd pitch his course, splitting the profits with his partners. Win-win!

The results? Mind-blowing. In just over a year, Joseph's email list exploded to 25,000 subscribers, and his course sales soared. Soon, he waved goodbye to his 9-to-5 and hello to full-time entrepreneurship.[13]

Joseph's story isn't just inspiring - it's a blueprint for success. This chapter is your guide to leveraging partnerships and rapidly growing your audience. We're talking rocket fuel for your email list!

Why does this matter? Simple. Partnerships accelerate your growth, skyrocketing you past the slow grind of solo efforts. They lend you instant credibility, putting you in front of eager, trusting audiences. And the best part? Everyone wins.

Ready to turn your side hustle into your main gig? Let's dive in and unlock the power of partner traffic!

The Partner Traffic Advantage

Ever feel like you're shouting into the void? That's solo audience-building for you. But partner traffic? It's like borrowing a megaphone from a friend with a crowd already gathered.

Imagine tapping into established audiences overnight—no more crickets chirping at your content. You're suddenly center stage, with all eyes on you. It's like being the opening act for a rock star—their fans become your fans.

Here's the kicker: you're not just borrowing an audience; you're borrowing trust. Your partner's seal of approval is golden. Their audience thinks, "If he or she says this is good, it must be!" Instant credibility boost.

But wait, there's more! This isn't a one-way street. You're creating win-win relationships. Your partners get fresh content; you get exposure. They earn commissions; you gain subscribers. It's like a business potluck where everyone brings something to the table and leaves satisfied.

And talk about fast-tracking your success! Your email list? It'll grow faster than a kid in a growth spurt. Revenue potential? The sky's the limit. You're not just climbing the ladder of success - you're taking the express elevator.

Think about it. Which is better? Spending months (or years) to build an audience from scratch? Or leveraging partnerships to reach thousands of ideal customers almost instantly?

Partner traffic isn't just smart. It's rocket fuel for your business growth. Ready to light that fuse?

Method 1: The Email Swap Strategy

Let's kick things off with a simple yet powerful strategy: the email swap. It's like trading baseball cards. You're swapping valuable content and subscribers instead of cardboard.

Step 1: Develop an Irresistible Lead Magnet

First things first, you need bait - and not just any bait. We're talking about the kind of offer that makes people stop scrolling and think, "I need that!"

Create a high-value PDF resource. This could be a checklist, guide, template, or cheat sheet. Whatever form it takes, make sure it solves a specific problem for your target audience. It should be like a slice of cake at a bakery - a free taste that leaves them craving more.

Your lead magnet needs to be easily digestible and immediately actionable. There should be no fluff or filler—just pure, problem-solving goodness. Remember, you're not writing a novel here. You're creating a resource that people can use right away to get results.

Step 2: Craft Partner-Perspective Emails

Now, let's make life easy for your partners. Write 1-3 emails from their perspective, highlighting the value of your lead magnet to their audience. This is your chance to shine - show off your lead magnet's benefits and make it irresistible.

Provide these emails as swipe copy to your partners. They should be able to copy, paste, and hit send with minimal effort. As Russell Brunson says, "The key to successful partnerships is making it as effortless as possible for your partners to promote you."

Step 3: Implement the Email Swap Strategy

It's time to find your swap buddies. Look for potential partners with email lists similar in size to yours. Don't be shy - reach out and propose a mutual email promotion arrangement.

Here's how it works: You send an email promoting their lead magnet to your list, and they do the same for you. It's like introducing your friends to each other at a party - everyone benefits from expanded connections.

Remember, this isn't a one-time deal. Build relationships with your swap partners. The more you swap, the more your list grows. And who knows? Today's swap partner might be tomorrow's joint venture collaborator.

Method 2: The Guest Teacher Strategy

Ready to step into the spotlight? The Guest Teacher Strategy is your ticket to center stage. It's like being the cool substitute teacher everyone loves - you sweep in, drop knowledge bombs, and leave the audience wanting more.

Step 1: Develop a Compelling Webinar Presentation

First up, craft a webinar that'll knock their socks off. Create slides that pop and showcase your expertise. Think visually appealing and easy to follow. Your content should be a value bomb, giving attendees immediate takeaways they can use.

Structure your presentation like a three-act play. Open with a bang, deliver the goods, and smoothly transition to your paid offer. Remember Amy Porterfield's words: "A great webinar is not a sales pitch. It's a valuable learning experience that leaves the audience wanting more."

Step 2: Craft Partner Promotion Emails for Your Webinar

Now, let's get people excited about your webinar. Write an email copy your partners can send to their lists. Highlight what makes your webinar unique. Why should people attend? What will they learn? Make it irresistible!

Include clear calls to action for registration. Make it easy for people to say yes. Your partner promotion emails should be like movie trailers—exciting glimpses that make people eager to see the full feature.

Step 3: Reach Out to Potential Partners

Time to find your co-stars. Research and identify influencers in your niche who align with your values and audience. Personalize your outreach messages. Show them you've done your homework and understand their audience.

Clearly communicate the mutual benefits of partnership. What's in it for them? As Richard Branson says, "The best partnerships are built on a foundation of shared values and complementary strengths." Make sure they see the win-win.

Step 4: Execute and Optimize Your Partner Traffic Strategies

Lights, camera, action! Implement your email swaps and guest webinars. But don't just set it and forget it. Track your results meticulously. Gather feedback from partners and attendees.

Use this data to refine your approach continuously. Optimizing your partner traffic strategies is like tuning a race car. Minor adjustments can greatly improve performance. Keep tweaking until you're zooming past the competition.

Remember, each webinar is a chance to grow your list and revenue. Even if sales are slow initially, you're building an audience of interested prospects. Keep delivering value, and the results will follow.

Today's Exercise: Kickstart Your Email Swap Strategy

Ready to dip your toes into the email swap pool? Let's start with a focused, one-day exercise to set the foundation for your first swap.

1. Brainstorm Lead Magnet Ideas

What valuable, quick-win resource could you create for your audience? A checklist? A template? A short guide? Aim for at least 5-7 ideas.

2. Choose Your Lead Magnet

Review your list. Which idea excites you most? Which one could you create quickly? Which would provide the most value to your audience? Pick one. This is your lead magnet.

3. Identify Potential Swap Partners

It's Time to play matchmaker. Who in your niche has an email list that is similar to yours? Look for complementary offerings, not direct competitors. Aim to list 5-10 potential partners. Check their websites, social media, or podcast directories to find them.

4. Draft Your Outreach Email

Craft a friendly, personalized email to propose the swap. Keep it short and sweet. Here's a basic structure:

- Greeting and personal connection (if any)

- Brief introduction of yourself and your audience

- Proposal of the email swap idea

- Mention your lead magnet and its value

- Ask if they'd be interested in discussing further

- Thank them for their time

Remember, this is just a draft. You'll personalize it for each potential partner later.

Congratulations! You've laid the groundwork for your email swap strategy. You've got your lead magnet idea, a list of potential partners, and an outreach email template. You're well on your way to growing your audience through partnerships. Next step? Create that lead magnet and start reaching out. You've got this!

Key Takeaways:

- Partner traffic strategies can quickly grow your audience and email list. These include email swaps and guest webinars.

- Success in partner traffic requires high-value lead magnets and great presentations. It's also key to make it easy for partners to promote you.

- Successful, sustainable partner traffic strategies rely on mutual benefits. They must build genuine relationships.

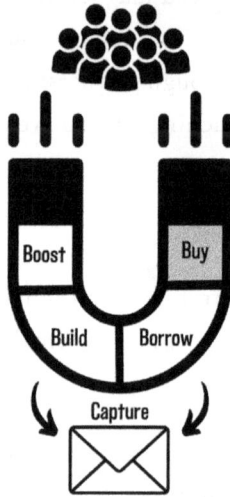

The Buy Method
(Paid Traffic)

19

The Paid Traffic Playbook (Lead Campaigns)

A small digital magazine decides to launch an Instagram course. They're not exactly household names. But they have a secret weapon: Facebook ads.

Foundr Magazine had a hunch. They knew entrepreneurs were itching to crack the Instagram code, so they whipped up some free training videos. Nothing fancy, just solid, actionable tips. Then, they fired up Facebook's ad machine.

Here's where it gets wild.

In just three months, they poured $100,000 into Facebook ads. Sounds like a lot, right? But hold onto your hats. Those ads? They brought in a whopping 250,000 new email subscribers.

Let that sink in. A quarter million people raised their hands and said, "Yes, teach me!"

But it gets better. When Foundr finally launched its course, it didn't just do well—it knocked it out of the park. We're talking $1.3 million in revenue from their very first launch![14]

Now, I know what you're thinking. "That's great for them, but I don't have $100,000 lying around!"

Breathe easy. You don't need that kind of cash to see results. The principles work whether you're spending $100 or $100,000. It's all about strategy, not just throwing money at the problem.

In this chapter, we'll explore the world of Facebook lead campaigns. We'll uncover the secrets of Foundr's successful campaign. Then, we'll show you how to use those same principles on a tight budget.

Ready to turn on the tap and watch your email list grow? Let's dive in.

The Facebook Ad Fumble: Common Mistakes and How to Avoid Them

Let's talk about what most people do when they dip their toes into Facebook ads. It's like jumping into the deep end without knowing how to swim.

They dive in headfirst, no life jacket in sight. There's no real plan, just a vague hope that throwing money at ads will magically bring in customers. Sound familiar?

These folks usually start small. They set a daily budget of $10 or $25, thinking it's enough to make a splash. But here's the kicker: panic sets in after just a few days. Where are all the sales? Why isn't anyone buying?

By day four or five, they're ready to give up. The ads are shut off faster than you can say "Facebook pixel." And just like that, paid advertising is written off as a waste of money.

But here's why this approach is about as practical as trying to fill a bucket with a hole in it:

- There's no patience. Building an audience takes time, but

most people expect overnight success.

- Expectations are way off. They're looking for immediate sales when they should be focused on building relationships.

- They're missing the big picture. An email list is a goldmine, but they're too focused on quick wins to see it.

So, what's the better way? It's time to flip the script.

First, approach paid traffic like a chess game, not a slot machine. You need a strategy, not just hope and a prayer.

Next, set aside a real advertising budget and treat it like any other business expense. It's not money down the drain; it's an investment in your future.

Here's the key: focus on lead generation, not immediate sales. Your goal is to build an army of interested prospects, not to make a quick buck.

Finally, change your mindset. Paid advertising isn't an expense—it's an investment. You're buying future revenue, not just clicks.

The Lead Campaign Launchpad: Your 7-Step Strategy for Success

Ready to turn your Facebook ad campaign into a lead-generating machine? Here are seven manageable steps.

1. Set Your Budget

First things first: decide how much you're willing to invest. This isn't about immediate returns. Think of it like planting seeds in a garden.

You're investing upfront, nurturing over time, and eventually reaping a bountiful harvest.

How much can you comfortably allocate without expecting instant results? Calculate your potential ROI based on your customers' lifetime value. Remember, you're playing the long game here.

2. Define Your Target Cost Per Lead

Know your numbers. Research what others in your industry are paying per lead. Then, set a realistic goal based on your offer and audience.

E.W. Deming said it best: "He who knows his numbers knows his business." So get cozy with your calculator. Your future self will thank you.

3. Craft Your Lead Magnet

It's time to create something irresistible. What free offer can you develop that addresses your audience's pain points? Make sure it aligns with your paid products or services.

Think of your lead magnet as a free sample at a grocery store. It gives potential customers a taste of what you offer and leaves them hungry for more.

4. Design Your Landing Page

Keep it simple, focused, and distraction-free. Your landing page has one job: to capture email addresses. Include clear benefits and a strong call to action.

Leonardo da Vinci wasn't talking about landing pages when he said, "Simplicity is the ultimate sophistication." But he might as well have been.

5. Set Up Your Facebook Ad Campaign

It's time to roll up your sleeves and dive into the Facebook Ads Manager. Think of this as your command center. You're about to launch a mission to capture leads; every detail matters.

First, choose the "Conversions" objective. This tells Facebook you're after leads, not just likes or views.

Now that you've set your conversion objective, it's time to tackle the most crucial part of your Facebook ad strategy: picking your audience. This isn't just about who you think might like your product. It's about understanding the different types of audiences and choosing the right one for your campaign.

Let's break it down:

Warm Audience

These are the folks who already know you. They're your email subscribers, social media followers, or website visitors. They've shown interest in what you do. Think of them as your fan club. They're more likely to engage with your ads because they already know your brand.

Cold Audience

This group doesn't know you... yet. They're strangers but potential friends. You're targeting them based on demographics (age, location, gender), psychographics (interests, behaviors), or cold interests (liked pages, engaged topics). It's like introducing yourself at a party where you don't know anyone.

Lookalike Audience

Here's where things get interesting. Lookalike audiences are cold audiences that "look like" your warm audience. Facebook takes a group you know (like your email list) and finds people with similar characteristics. It's like asking your friends to introduce you to their friends. The possibilities are nearly endless, but don't worry – we'll focus on the most effective ones.

So, which audience should you choose?

Here's a pro tip: Start with your warm audience. These people already know you, so they're more likely to respond positively to your ads. It's like preaching to the choir – they're primed to listen.

Beginning with a warm audience allows you to test your ad copy, images, and offers with a friendly crowd. You can gather data, see what works, and refine your approach before venturing into colder waters.

Now for the fun part: creating your ad. Remember, you're not just making an ad; you're crafting an invitation. Your ad should stop the scroll and spark curiosity.

Here's an example from one of my best-performing ads:

> Want to start a blog but don't know where to start?
> Grab our 9-page Discover Your Blog Niche Blueprint PDF, and you'll know which blog topic is right for you!
> Learn More: http://MarketYourMessage.com/Discover"

See how it works? It starts with a question that directly addresses the audience's pain point. Then, it offers a solution—a free PDF guide. Finally, it ends with a clear call to action.

For your image, use something eye-catching that relates to your offer. A picture of someone looking frustrated at a computer could work well for our blog example.

Don't forget your headline:

> FREE DOWNLOAD: The Discover Your Blog Niche Blueprint

Setting up your campaign is like casting a net. The better you aim, the more likely you are to catch your target audience. So take your time, be precise, and get ready to reel in those leads!

6. Monitor and Optimize

Track key metrics like cost per lead, click-through, and conversion rates. A/B tests different ad elements to improve performance.

Peter Drucker nailed it: "What gets measured gets managed." So keep a close eye on those numbers.

7. Nurture Your Leads

Develop an email sequence to build relationships with your new subscribers. Provide value and gradually introduce your paid offerings.

Nurturing leads is like tending to a garden. Consistent care and attention lead to growth and fruitful results.

There you have it. Your roadmap to Facebook ad success. Ready to start your journey?

Today's Exercise: Write Your First Lead Campaign Ad

Ready to put your newfound knowledge into action? Today, we're going to craft your very first lead campaign ad. Don't worry, we'll take it step by step. Grab a pen and paper, or open a new document on your computer. Let's dive in!

1. Define Your Offer

What free value can you provide? Is it a PDF guide, a video series, or a mini-course? Jot down your idea.

2. Identify Your Audience

Who would benefit most from your offer? Describe your ideal lead in a few sentences.

3. Craft Your Headline

Write a punchy headline that grabs attention. Remember our example: "FREE DOWNLOAD: The Discover Your Blog Niche Blueprint."

4. Draft Your Ad Copy

Use this structure:

- Ask a compelling question

- Highlight the benefit of your free offer

- Include a clear call to action

Here's a template to get you started:

> Are you struggling with [problem]?
> Grab our free [type of content] and learn how to [benefit].
> Click here to download now: [LINK.]

5. Choose Your Image

Describe or sketch an image that would complement your ad. Remember, it should be eye-catching and relevant to your offer.

6. Set Your Budget

Decide on a daily budget you're comfortable with. Even $5-$10 per day is a great start.

7. Plan Your Landing Page

Outline what you want on your landing page. Keep it simple: a headline, a brief description of your offer, and an email sign-up form.

Congratulations! You've just created the blueprint for your first lead campaign ad. Take a moment to review and refine your work.

Remember, this is just the beginning. As you launch and run your campaign, you'll continually gather data and insights to improve your ads. But for now, pat yourself on the back. You've taken a huge step towards mastering Facebook lead campaigns!

Key Takeaways:

- Approach Facebook lead campaigns as a long-term investment in building your email list, not as a quick way to generate sales.

- Set a budget for ads. Set realistic cost-per-lead targets. This will help you avoid getting discouraged by short-term results.

- Create valuable lead magnets. Optimize your landing pages. Nurture your leads. This will maximize your ad ROI.

20

The Paid Traffic Playbook (Sales Campaigns)

I t's 1886. Atlanta is buzzing with the usual hustle and bustle. But in a small pharmacy, something extraordinary is brewing. A local pharmacist, John Pemberton, has just concocted a syrup that'll change the world. He calls it Coca-Cola.

But here's the problem: nobody knows about it yet.

Pemberton's got a game-changing drink, but it might as well be snake oil without customers. So what does he do? He takes a bold step. He scrapes together $20 - a hefty sum in those days - and buys his very first advertisement.

It's a risk. A big one. Will anyone even notice? Will they care? Pemberton's probably sweating bullets as he waits to see what happens.

It was a gamble. But boy, did it pay off! That single ad raked in $50 in sales. A 150% return on investment. Not too shabby, right?

This wasn't just a win for Pemberton. It was the start of something big. That $20 ad kicked off a marketing revolution. It showed the world the power of advertising done right.[15]

Fast-forward to today. We're not placing ads in newspapers anymore. We're running Facebook campaigns and wrestling with algorithms. But the core idea? It's still the same: Smart advertising can turn a small investment into big returns.

But here's the kicker: most people get it wrong. They expect every ad to be like Pemberton's - an instant hit. They think they'll put in $10 and magically get $100 back. Spoiler alert: that's not how it usually works.

In this chapter, we're going to bust some myths. We'll look at what most people do with their Facebook ad campaigns, why it doesn't work, and, most importantly, what you should do instead.

Ready to revolutionize your approach to paid traffic? Let's dive in.

The Great Ad Expectations: Why Instant Results Are a Mirage

Let's discuss what most people do when they dive into Facebook ad campaigns. They're like kids on Christmas morning, eyes wide with excitement, expecting miracles. They toss $10 into the Facebook machine and sit back, waiting for $100 to come rolling in. Sounds great, right?

But here's the thing: they panic when those instant results don't show up.

They pull the plug faster than you can say "algorithm." It's like planting a seed and digging it up daily to see if it's grown. Spoiler alert: it hasn't, and it won't if you don't give it time.

These folks are missing a crucial point. Facebook's algorithm isn't a magician—it's more like a very smart student. It needs time to learn and figure out who's most likely to buy your stuff.

But when you cut the campaign short, you're basically tearing up the algorithm's homework before it's finished.

Why doesn't this work?

Well, for starters, those sky-high expectations are a recipe for disappointment. When reality doesn't match the dream, people get discouraged and miss out on potential goldmines. It's like giving up on a marathon because you're not in first place after the first mile.

Another big no-no is yanking campaigns too soon. Remember our student algorithm? By ending things prematurely, you're not giving it a chance to graduate. It needs time to learn, improve, and eventually decrease advertising costs. And let's not forget the bigger picture.

That person who clicked on your ad today? They might not buy right away, but they could become a loyal customer down the line. Short-term thinking misses this long-game potential. So what should you do instead?

It's time for a mindset shift. Think of your ad spend as an investment, not an expense. Your goal? Break-even at first. Sounds boring, I know, but hear me out.

Aiming to break even gives you (and that hardworking algorithm) time to learn and improve. You're building a customer base - and that's worth its weight in gold. These are people who might buy from you again and again. Give it time. Let the algorithm do its thing. Focus on the long game. It might not be as exciting as instant riches, but trust me, it's a whole lot more sustainable.

Cracking the Code: 5 Steps to Facebook Ad Success

1. Set Realistic Goals

First things first: let's get real about your goals. Forget about those pie-in-the-sky dreams of 10x returns right off the bat. Instead, aim to break even. For every $100 you spend on ads, shoot for $100 in sales. Sounds boring? It's not. It's smart.

This approach is like planting a tree. A Chinese proverb says, "The best time to plant a tree was 20 years ago. The second best time is now."

Your ad campaign is that tree. You're not looking for fruit today. You're building a strong root system - a solid customer base that'll pay off soon.

2. Master the Art of Retargeting

Let's talk about the Facebook pixel. If you haven't heard of it, buckle up because this little piece of code will become your secret weapon. It's like a digital spy, quietly gathering intel on everyone who visits your website.

And trust me, that information is pure gold.

Here's what you do: Install the Facebook pixel on your website—every page, no exceptions. It's easy—just a bit of copy-paste magic in your site's header.

Once there, it starts working its magic, tracking every visitor.

Now, here's where it gets interesting. Set up a custom audience for your sales page. This tells Facebook, "Hey, keep an eye on anyone who lands on this specific page."

These are your hot leads - people who've shown real interest in what you're selling.

But why stop there?

Create custom audiences for different product pages, your About page, and even your blog posts. Each of these audiences represents a different level of interest and a different stage in the customer journey.

Now, let's put this into action. Say you're selling a course on digital marketing. Someone visits your sales page but doesn't buy. No problem. You can now show them an ad that says something like:

> Still wondering if our Digital Marketing Mastery course is right for you?
> Here's what Sarah B. had to say: 'This course took my business from struggling to six figures in just six months!'
> Ready to transform your business?
> Click here for a special offer!

This isn't random advertising. This is laser-focused messaging to someone who's already interested. It's like spotting a customer lingering near a product in your store, walking over, and saying, "You know, that item is on sale today. And by the way, it comes with this cool bonus feature."

Retargeting is powerful because it's personal. It's not pushy; it's helpful. You're not interrupting someone's day with a random ad. You're following up on a genuine interest they've already shown.

And here's a pro tip: Don't just retarget with sales messages.

You should also try to:

- Mix it up.

- Share a helpful blog post.

- Offer a free guide.

- Show them a video testimonial.

Keep providing value; you'll stay top-of-mind until they're ready to buy.

Remember, in the world of online marketing, attention is currency. Retargeting helps you make the most of the attention you've already earned. It's not just smart marketing - it's respectful marketing.

You're continuing a conversation that your potential customer has already started.

3. Embrace Low-Dollar Front-End Offers

Let's flip the script on traditional sales thinking. Instead of going for the big sale right off the bat, we will start small—really small.

We're talking about creating an offer so irresistible that it's almost a no-brainer for your potential customers.

Here's the strategy: Create a high-value, low-cost product.

We're aiming for the sweet spot between $7 and $17. At this price point, people are willing to take a chance.

It's low risk for them but a high reward for you.

Let's say you're a business coach. You could create a mini-course called "Launch Pad: 5-Day Business Starter Kit" and price it at $17.

This course is packed with value - step-by-step training videos, worksheets, and a private Facebook group for support.

It's a taste of what you offer, but it stands alone as a valuable product.

Now, here's what your ad might look like:

Dreaming of starting your own business but feeling lost? Turn your passion into profit in just five days!
Introducing "Launch Pad: 5-Day Business Starter Kit" - your fast track to entrepreneurship.

- 5 video modules on business essentials

- Customizable business plan template

- Access to our 'Future Founders' community

All for only $17! That's less than a business book but way more interactive.
Learn how to:

- Validate your business idea

- Identify your target market

- Create a basic marketing plan

- Understand startup financials

- Pitch your idea effectively

Don't let another year slip by. Your business journey starts now!
Click to grab your 'Launch Pad' and take off in 5 days!

This ad works because it:

1. Speaks to a common desire (starting a business)

2. Offers a structured, time-bound solution

3. Provides tangible, valuable resources

4. Uses the low price as a selling point

5. Breaks down the key learnings

6. Creates a sense of urgency and excitement

Remember, this low-dollar offer is your foot in the door. It's not about making a profit on this product. It's about gaining a customer's trust and showing your expertise. This sets the stage for future, higher-ticket sales. You're not just selling a course but opening a relationship with a potential long-term customer.

This strategy isn't just about making sales. It's about building a loyal customer base, one $17 offer at a time. It's playing the long game, and in the world of online marketing, that's how you win.

4. Get Savvy with Strategic Upsells

Once you've hooked a customer with your low-dollar offer, it's time to reel them in. Offer one or two relevant upsells at higher price points. But here's the key: make sure these upsells add real value.

It's like when you order a burger, and they ask if you want fries. The fries complement the burger, making your meal better. Yours should do the same - enhance the customer's experience while boosting your bottom line.

5. Keep Your Eye on the Ball: Monitor and Optimize

Last but not least, you've got to stay on your toes. Regularly check your campaign's vital signs: cost per acquisition, click-through rate, and conversion rate. Use this data to fine-tune your targeting, tweak your ad creative, and adjust your offers.

Remember, success in Facebook advertising isn't about overnight riches. It's about playing the long game, building relationships, and constantly learning. Stick with this plan, and you'll be well on your way to mastering the art of paid traffic.

Today's Exercise: Write Your First Sales Ad

Today, we're going to create your very first Facebook sales ad. Don't worry if you've never done this – we'll take it step by step.

1. Define Your Offer: What's your low-dollar product or service? It should be priced between $7-$17. Write it down along with its key benefits.

2. Identify Your Target Audience: Who would benefit most from your offer? Be specific. Consider age, interests, and pain points.

3. Craft Your Headline: Write a catchy, benefit-driven headline in 5-7 words. Make it scroll-stopping!

4. List Key Features: Jot down 3-5 main features or benefits of your offer. Use bullet points for clarity.

5. Create Urgency: How can you make people want to buy now? Limited time offer? Are limited spots available?

6. Call-to-Action: What exact action do you want people to take? "Buy Now"? "Sign Up Today"? Make it clear and compelling.

7. Write Your Ad Copy: Now, combine all these elements into a short, punchy ad. Aim for about 100-150 words.

8. Add Visuals: Describe or sketch a simple image comple-

menting your ad. Remember, visuals grab attention!

9. Review and Refine: Read your ad aloud. Does it flow? Is it clear? Make any necessary tweaks.

10. Plan Your Testing: Write down 2-3 variations you could test (e.g., different headlines, images, or CTAs).

Congratulations! You've just created the blueprint for your first sales ad. This exercise gives you a practical ad to use and helps you think through the key elements of effective advertising. Remember, the goal isn't perfection – it's progress. You'll refine and improve as you go along.

Ready to see your ad in action? The next step is to set up your Facebook ad account and bring this ad to life!

Key Takeaways:

- Patience pays: Focus on breaking even and building your customer base while the algorithm learns.

- Maximize value: Use retargeting, low-dollar offers, and strategic upsells to acquire customers profitably.

- Monitor and optimize. Analyze key metrics to boost performance and grow.

21

The Build Your Audience 60-Day Action Plan

C ongratulations on completing your journey through "Build Your Audience!"

You should feel proud of taking this important first step towards turning your ideas into a thriving online community. It's normal to feel a bit uncertain as you begin to implement the strategies you've learned, but remember that your unique perspective and solutions matter.

Your approach has the potential to help and inspire others facing similar challenges in building their own audiences. Focus on serving those who need your insights and guidance the most. Create content from the heart, regardless of the current size of your following. Many of history's most influential creators started small before their work caught fire based on the value they provided.

You now have all the tools needed to overcome common hurdles that new content creators face. This book has equipped you to handle various aspects of audience building, from identifying your niche to engaging with your community effectively. Whenever self-doubt creeps in, recall the strategies and advice contained in these pages.

Your dream of impacting lives through your content is absolutely within reach. Our world needs more authentic voices and innovators - exactly what you offer. Feel optimistic knowing that everything that brought you to this point has prepared you for what comes next.

I applaud you for undertaking this fulfilling yet challenging path of audience building. Now, go forth and make your unique mark in the digital world!

If you prefer working through this material with a physical companion, be sure to check out the "Build Your Audience Companion Workbook." This supplementary guide contains all the exercises from the book in a convenient print format. Completing them with pen and paper can help reinforce the lessons even more.

You can refer back to the workbook whenever you need motivation or want to revisit the core principles that will empower your audience-building journey. Having an offline reference helps many people process, retain, and apply these essential concepts more effectively.

You can learn more at PlatformGrowthBooks.com.

Whether you choose to continue with the digital version or pick up the workbook, you now hold the keys to building a successful and engaged audience!

The Build Your Audience 60-Day Action Plan

First, choose your own traffic adventure below. Then, focus on implementing the recommended tasks and goals over eight weeks (60 days) to see results. Work on only one traffic method at a time. Good luck!

The Daily Post Traffic Playbook:

- Week 1: Choose your primary social media platform and develop a content calendar

- Week 2: Create and schedule 1 post per day on your chosen platform

- Week 3: Analyze engagement and refine your content strategy

- Week 4: Increase posting frequency to 2-3 times per day

- Week 5: Experiment with different post types (text, images, videos, etc.)

- Week 6: Run a social media challenge or contest to boost engagement

- Week 7: Collaborate with others in your niche for cross-promotion

- Week 8: Review metrics and set new goals for continued growth

The Video Shorts Traffic Playbook

- Week 1: Choose your video platform (TikTok, Instagram Reels, YouTube Shorts)

- Week 2: Plan and create 5-7 short video ideas

- Week 3: Post 1 video per day and engage with others in your niche

- Week 4: Analyze performance and refine your video strategy

- Week 5: Experiment with different video styles and topics

- Week 6: Collaborate with other creators on joint videos

- Week 7: Run a video challenge or series to boost engagement

- Week 8: Review metrics and set new goals for video content

The Private Facebook Group Traffic Playbook

- Week 1: Set up your Facebook group and develop group rules/guidelines

- Week 2: Invite initial members and create a content calendar

- Week 3: Post daily and engage actively with members

- Week 4: Run your first group challenge or event

- Week 5: Analyze group insights and refine your strategy

- Week 6: Implement themed days (e.g. Motivation Monday, Q&A Friday)

- Week 7: Host a live video Q&A or training in the group

- Week 8: Review growth and set new goals for group engagement

The Blogging Traffic Playbook

- Week 1: Develop your blog content strategy and editorial calendar

- Week 2: Write and publish 2 high-quality blog posts

- Week 3: Optimize your posts for SEO and promote on social media

- Week 4: Guest post on 2-3 relevant blogs in your niche

- Week 5: Create a lead magnet to grow your email list

- Week 6: Implement internal linking and optimize older posts

- Week 7: Repurpose blog content into other formats (video, infographics, etc.)

- Week 8: Analyze traffic and set new content goals

The Medium Traffic Playbook

- Week 1: Set up your Medium profile and plan your content strategy

- Week 2: Publish 2-3 articles on Medium

- Week 3: Engage with others and submit to relevant publications

- Week 4: Analyze performance and refine your approach

- Week 5: Experiment with different article types and topics

- Week 6: Get featured in a major Medium publication

- Week 7: Cross-promote your Medium content on other platforms

- Week 8: Review growth and set new goals for Medium

The Podcast Traffic Playbook

- Week 1: Plan your podcast concept, format, and first few episodes

- Week 2: Record and edit your first 3-5 podcast episodes

- Week 3: Launch your podcast on major platforms (Apple, Spotify, etc.)

- Week 4: Promote your podcast on social media and to your email list

- Week 5: Invite your first podcast guest and conduct the interview

- Week 6: Implement show notes and transcripts for SEO

- Week 7: Cross-promote with other podcasters in your niche

- Week 8: Analyze listener data and set growth goals

The YouTube Traffic Playbook

- Week 1: Develop your YouTube channel strategy and branding

- Week 2: Create and upload your first 2-3 videos

- Week 3: Optimize video titles, descriptions, and tags for SEO

- Week 4: Engage with your audience and other creators in your niche

- Week 5: Experiment with different video types (how-to, vlogs, etc.)

- Week 6: Create and promote a flagship video series

- Week 7: Implement YouTube Shorts into your strategy

- Week 8: Analyze channel metrics and set new growth goals

The Pinterest Traffic Playbook

- Week 1: Set up your Pinterest business account and initial boards

- Week 2: Create and pin 20-30 pins for your content

- Week 3: Join and contribute to relevant group boards

- Week 4: Implement a consistent pinning schedule (10-25 pins daily)

- Week 5: Create Pinterest-specific graphics for your content

- Week 6: Experiment with different pin designs and strategies

- Week 7: Set up and run your first Pinterest ad campaign

- Week 8: Analyze traffic and refine your Pinterest strategy

The Guest Blogging Traffic Playbook

- Week 1: Sign up for HARO and prepare your expert profile

- Week 2: Monitor HARO for relevant queries matching your expertise

- Week 3: Craft and submit high-quality responses to 3-5 HARO queries

- Week 4: Follow up with journalists and monitor for publications

- Week 5: Promote any media mentions across your platforms

- Week 6: Connect with journalists on social media and engage with their content

- Week 7: Repurpose your HARO responses and media mentions for your own content

- Week 8: Analyze results and refine your HARO strategy for future outreach

The Guest Podcasting Traffic Playbook

- Week 1: Identify 20-30 relevant podcasts in your niche

- Week 2: Develop your guest podcasting pitch and topic ideas

- Week 3: Reach out and secure 3-5 podcast guest spots

- Week 4: Prepare for your podcast interviews (talking points, etc.)

- Week 5: Record your first 2-3 podcast guest appearances

- Week 6: Promote your podcast episodes to your audience

- Week 7: Create bonus content for podcast listeners

- Week 8: Follow up with hosts and analyze results

The Guest Video Interview Traffic Playbook

- Week 1: Identify 20-30 potential video interview opportunities

- Week 2: Develop your video interview pitch and topic ideas

- Week 3: Reach out and secure 3-5 video interview spots

- Week 4: Prepare your setup for professional video interviews

- Week 5: Conduct your first 2-3 video interviews

- Week 6: Promote your video interviews on all platforms

- Week 7: Repurpose interview content for other formats

- Week 8: Analyze results and refine your video interview strategy

The Guest Email Traffic Playbook

- Week 1: Identify 20-30 potential email newsletter partners

- Week 2: Develop your email guest content ideas and pitches

- Week 3: Reach out and secure 3-5 email newsletter features

- Week 4: Write your guest email content

- Week 5: Have your content featured in partner emails

- Week 6: Promote the partner newsletters to your audience

- Week 7: Follow up with new subscribers from partner lists

- Week 8: Analyze results and refine your email partnership strategy

The Paid Traffic Playbook (Lead Campaigns)

- Week 1: Define your lead magnet and target audience

- Week 2: Set up your lead capture page and thank you page

- Week 3: Create your ad creative (copy and visuals)

- Week 4: Set up and launch your first lead generation campaign

- Week 5: Monitor and optimize ad performance daily

- Week 6: Scale up successful ads and pause underperforming ones

- Week 7: Implement retargeting for non-converters

- Week 8: Analyze overall campaign performance and refine strategy

The Paid Traffic Playbook (Sales Campaigns)

- Week 1: Define your offer and ideal customer profile

- Week 2: Set up your sales page and checkout process

- Week 3: Create your ad creative (copy and visuals)

- Week 4: Set up and launch your first sales campaign

- Week 5: Monitor and optimize ad performance daily

- Week 6: Implement upsells and cross-sells in your funnel

- Week 7: Create a retargeting campaign for interested non-buyers

- Week 8: Analyze overall campaign performance and refine strategy

22
What's Next?

Congratulations on completing your journey through *"Build Your Audience"*! By now, you've mastered the art of attracting and engaging a loyal following that resonates with your message and vision.

But as you celebrate this milestone, you might be wondering, "What's next?" Now that you've successfully built your audience, where should you focus your energy to keep the momentum going and scale your impact?

Whenever my private clients ask this question, my response is always the same: "It's time to scale your income!"

You see, building an audience is a crucial step, but to truly grow a thriving business, you need to diversify your revenue streams and maximize your earning potential. And the key to doing that is by strategically creating multiple income streams around your core message.

But here's the thing: scaling your income can feel overwhelming, especially if you're new to product creation and business models. With so many options and strategies to choose from, it's easy to get stuck in analysis paralysis and fail to take consistent action.

That's why I've developed powerful frameworks to help any writer, coach, teacher, or speaker scale their income quickly and efficiently:

- The Messenger Product Map: Discover 12 income streams you can create from one core message.

- The Profit Pyramid: Learn how to craft mini, main, and max offers that cater to different segments of your audience.

- The Hub & Spoke Blueprint: A strategic plan to create 7 income streams in just 12 months.

Each of these frameworks, when implemented strategically, can help you transform your audience into a thriving, multi-faceted business. And the best part? You don't need to be a business guru or marketing genius to make them work for you.

Want to know the step-by-step playbook for implementing these frameworks and scaling your income to new heights?

That's exactly what I cover in depth in the next book of this series: "Scale Your Income: The 48-Day Income Blueprint to Create Multiple Streams of Revenue as a Writer, Coach, Teacher, or Speaker."

Inside, you'll discover:

- How to leverage your core message to create 12 different product offerings.

- The secret to crafting irresistible offers at every price point.

- A strategic roadmap for launching 7 income streams in just one year.

- Advanced strategies for maximizing your revenue and impact.

- And much more!

If you're ready to take your business to the next level and start generating multiple streams of income, then "Scale Your Income" is your essential guide.

Don't let your hard-earned audience go to waste. It's time to provide them with a variety of ways to engage with your expertise and watch your impact and income soar.

Grab your copy of "*Scale Your Income: The 48-Day Income Blueprint to Create Multiple Streams of Revenue as a Writer, Coach, Teacher, or Speaker*" today at PlatformGrowthBooks.com.

Your financial freedom is waiting. Let's go scale your income together!

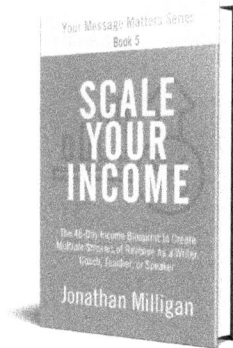

Thank You

I want to express my gratitude for choosing and purchasing my book. In a world overflowing with choices, you selected mine, and for that, I'm truly thankful.

Before we part ways, may I request a minor favor? Would it be too much to ask for you to leave a review on the platform? For an independent author like myself, receiving direct reader feedback through reviews significantly contributes to the success of the work.

Your insights will guide me in creating content that effectively aids you in achieving your desired results. Your feedback is highly valuable to me. Thank you for your time and consideration.

Leave a review by going to: **JMill.Biz/Build-Review**

1. Jamieson, Nikolas. "Blendtec's Viral Video Marketing Strategy Revealed." *Marketing Lab*, MarketingLab.com, https://marketinglab.com.au/blendtec-viral-video-marketing-strategy. Accessed 15 Aug. 2024.

2. Holiday, Ryan. "From Zero to 50,000: How I Built A Big Email List Exclusively About Books I Liked." *RyanHoliday.net*, https://ryanholiday.net/zero-to-50000-email-list-books. Accessed 15 Aug. 2024.

3. "The Fall of Troy: The Trojan Horse." *British Museum*, www.britishmuseum.org/learn/schools/ages-7-11/ancient-greece/the-myth-of-the-trojan-war. Accessed 15 Aug. 2024.

4. "Elisha Otis and the Invention of the Safety Elevator." *Britannica*, Encyclopaedia Britannica, https://www.britannica.com/biography/Elisha-Otis. Accessed 15 Aug. 2024.

5. "How Justin Welsh Built a $2M Solo Business on LinkedIn." *Digital Anfal*, www.digitalanfal.com/justin-welsh-linkedin-business. Accessed 15 Aug. 2024.

6. "Khaby Lame: From Factory Worker to TikTok Sensation and Global Icon." *Face2Face Africa*, 11 July 2024, https://face2faceafrica.com/article/khaby-lame-tiktok-sensation. Accessed 15 Aug. 2024.

7. "How Landon Stewart and Chris Stapleton Built Clients & Community from $2,000 to $10 Million." *Clients & Community*, https://clientsandcommunity.com/our-story. Accessed 15 Aug. 2024.

8. Hardy, Benjamin. "How I Used Medium to Get My First 20,000 Subscribers in 6 Months." *Goins, Writer*, https://goinswriter.com/medium-subscribers. Accessed 15 Aug. 2024.

9. "First Radio Transmission Sent Across the Atlantic Ocean." *H istory.com*, 11 Dec. 2023, https://www.history.com/this-day-in-h istory/marconi-sends-first-atlantic-wireless-transmission. Accessed 15 Aug. 2024.

10. "Cannell's Rise: From Small Church Videos to YouTube Success." *Bud Billion*, https://www.budbillion.com/sean-cannell-yo utube-success-think-media. Accessed 15 Aug. 2024.

11. "The 2020 Pinterest Algorithm Change and the Panic It Caused." *Confessions of a Food Blogger*, 15 Aug. 2024, https://www.confessionsofafoodblogger.com/2020-pinter est-algorithm-change. Accessed 15 Aug. 2024.

12. "Chicken Soup for the Soul: From Rejection to Bestseller." *Chicken Soup for the Soul*, https://www.chickensoup.com/history. Accessed 15 Aug. 2024.

13. "How Joseph Michael Built a Successful Scrivener Course and Became an Entrepreneur." *The Creative Penn*, https://www.thecreativepenn.com/joseph-michael-scriv ener-course-success. Accessed 15 Aug. 2024.

14. "How Foundr Magazine Used Facebook Ads to Launch a $1.3M Instagram Course." *Foundr*, https://www.foundr.com/how-foun dr-makes-its-millions. Accessed 15 Aug. 2024.

15. "Coca-Cola's First Advertisements and the Birth of a Global Brand." *History Oasis*, www.historyoasis.com/coca-cola-first-a dvertisements. Accessed 15 Aug. 2024.